YOU HAVE TO LIVE HARD TO BE HARD

ONE MAN'S LIFE IN SPECIAL OPERATIONS

DAN LAGUNA
CHIEF WARRANT OFFICER 4 (USA, RET.)

with MICHAEL S. WREN

authorHOUSE®

AuthorHouse™
1663 Liberty Drive
Bloomington, IN 47403
www.authorhouse.com
Phone: 1-800-839-8640

©2010 Dan Laguna with Michael S. Wren. All rights reserved.

No part of this book may be reproduced, stored in a retrieval system, or transmitted by any means without the written permission of the author.

First published by AuthorHouse   12/6/2010

ISBN: 978-1-4490-8123-2 (sc)
ISBN: 978-1-4490-8124-9 (hc)
ISBN: 978-1-4490-8125-6 (e)

Library of Congress Control Number: 2010917530

Printed in the United States of America

Any people depicted in stock imagery provided by Thinkstock are models, and such images are being used for illustrative purposes only. Certain stock imagery © Thinkstock.

This book is printed on acid-free paper.

Because of the dynamic nature of the Internet, any Web addresses or links contained in this book may have changed since publication and may no longer be valid. The views expressed in this work are solely those of the author and do not necessarily reflect the views of the publisher, and the publisher hereby disclaims any responsibility for them.

DEDICATION

Dedicated to my good friend, Carlos Guerrero, who died in the helicopter crash I survived on July 20, 1994, and to my brothers in arms, Arthur Laguna, Casey Cassavant, Shane Stanfield, Ron Johnson, and Steve Gernet, who died January 23rd, 2007, flying a combat rescue mission in Baghdad, Iraq, in support of a U.S. State Department Diplomat as contractors for Blackwater USA.

ACKNOWLEDGMENTS

I WOULD LIKE TO EXPRESS my thanks to Mike Wren, who helped me write this book. Although I had written about my life, it was in documentary form and not interesting at all to read and had no story line. He is the one who took my writings and turned them into a story. Without him, this book would not be.

Michael S. Wren and his wife, Sharon, are the parents of eight children and twenty-one grandchildren. Michael received a Bachelor of Science degree from Central Washington University and previously authored the book *Faith Under Fire*, also a true story about love and war. As an Army veteran, patriot, and constitutionalist, he has a strong appreciation for those who have shown valor in the defense of our nation and for the families at home who sacrifice in other ways to lend support to our defenders of freedom. Michael and Sharon currently reside in Eagle Mountain, Utah.

The Soldier's Prayer
PERSONALIZED FROM
PSALMS 91

He that dwelleth in the secret place of the most High shall abide
under the shadow of the Almighty. He will say of the Lord,
"He is my refuge and my fortress and my God; in Him will I Trust.
Surely He shall deliver me from the snare of the fowler,
and from the noisome pestilence.
He shall cover me with His feathers,
and under His wings shall I trust.
His truth shall be my shield and buckler.
I shall not be afraid for the terror by night;
Nor for the arrow that flieth by day;
Nor for the pestilence that walketh in darkness;
Nor for the destruction that wasteth at noonday.
A thousand shall fall at my side,
and ten thousand at my right hand;
But it shall not come nigh me.
Because I have made the Lord my refuge,
even the most High my habitation,
There shall no evil befall me.
Neither shall any plague come nigh my dwelling,
For He shall give His angels charge over me,
To keep me in all His ways.
The angels shall bear me up in their hands,
lest I dash my foot against a stone.
I shall tread upon the lion and adder;
The young lion and the dragon shalt I trample under my feet."
The Lord of Salvation shall say:
Because he hath set his love upon Me, I will deliver him.
I will set him on high, because he hath known my name.
He shall call upon Me, and I will answer him:
I will be with him in trouble;
I will deliver him, and honour him.
With long life will I satisfy him and shew him My salvation.

Special Forces Prayer
Almighty God, Who art the Author of liberty

And the Champion of the oppressed, hear our prayer.
We, the men of Special Forces, acknowledge
Our dependence upon Thee in the preservation of human freedom.
Go with us as we seek to defend the defenseless and to free the

Enslaved.
May we ever remember that our nation, whose motto
Is "in God We Trust", expects that we shall acquit
Ourselves with honor, that we may never bring shame

Upon our faith, our families, or our fellow men.
Grant us wisdom from Thy mind, courage from Thine

Heart, strength from Thine arm, and protection by Thine hand.
It is for Thee that we do battle, and to Thee belongs the victor's

Crown.
For Thine is the kingdom, and the power and the glory, forever.
AMEN

Contents

DEDICATION v
ACKNOWLEDGMENTS vii
FOREWORD xiii
PROLOGUE xvii
CHAPTER ONE Art's Funeral 1
CHAPTER TWO Little Bird Down 9
CHAPTER THREE Reflections of Youth 43
CHAPTER FOUR Army Life 57
CHAPTER FIVE Special Forces 71
CHAPTER SIX Flight School 83
CHAPTER SEVEN Desert Storm 95
CHAPTER EIGHT Mogadishu 103
CHAPTER NINE Events Leading To The Accident 113
CHAPTER TEN The Accident 123
CHAPTER ELEVEN Burn Unit (BAMC) 157
CHAPTER TWELVE Recovery at BACH 175
CHAPTER THIRTEEN Physical Therapy 189
CHAPTER FOURTEEN Flying Again 197
CHAPTER FIFTEEN More Surgery 205
CHAPTER SIXTEEN Operations In Baghdad 209
CHAPTER SEVENTEEN More Memories of Art 221
CHAPTER EIGHTEEN Miracles 225
CHAPTER NINETEEN Another Happy Day 231
APPENDIX *Arthur Laguna*..*235*

FOREWORD

Dan grew up in a small town outside Sacramento, California. He and his family were among the few minorities in our area. Back in the 60's, people were quite prejudiced. Most people thought of the minorities as people who would never amount to much. High school teachers would make comments to indicate as much. Instead of letting those comments make him angry, Dan used them as motivation. He would show them.

I was sixteen years old when I met Dan and started dating him. We married three years later. I have never regretted it. What I love about Dan is that he is strong and gentle at the same time. Dan is the most kind, gentle, loving, and forgiving person you will ever meet. I have never seen anyone who had so many friends. Everyone knows Dan or has heard of him in the Special Operations community. Once you become his friend you are a friend for life. His loyalty and integrity are beyond measure.

We have five children and he is the best father anyone could have. He loved to play with them when they were little and would joke around with them, as they grew older. He was strict but loving. There will never be a better father or husband than Dan, at least not for me.

Dan is a very strong-willed person and will stop at nothing, with all honesty and integrity, to achieve what he wants to do. No matter what he is trying to accomplish, whether it is building a deck, doing landscaping or whatever the case may be, it takes him three times longer to do it because of the perfection he puts into it. If something is hard to do, he doesn't give up. He will not quit until the task is accomplished. Over the years I have heard him tell our kids time and again "Lagunas aren't quitters." He will tell you that he isn't going to let his problems beat him. He is not satisfied unless the job is done to perfection. It seems everything is a competition in his eyes and he is going to do whatever it takes to win.

You have probably heard the saying, that if you want something done, you should give it to a busy person and they will get it done. That is true of Dan. He is a very busy person, but if you want something accomplished, just give it to him and he will kill himself trying to accomplish it.

These qualities have carried him far. After Dan had his helicopter accident on July 20, 1994, I realized he was much more the man than I ever imagined. He was in so much pain for months but he never complained or asked, "Why me?" He cried, but it wasn't for himself, it was for Carlos. His best friend, Carlos, died in the helicopter crash. Dan's 'life won't beat me' attitude carried him through the healing and recovery process. He was told he wouldn't fly again and would probably not walk without a cane or some kind of walking device. He proved everyone wrong including his doctors and psychiatrist. He always had a good attitude.

Nearly thirteen years later he would be tested beyond comprehension once again. Dan lost his brother, Arthur Laguna, as well as four other brave men he considered his brothers while on a combat mission in Baghdad. His determination to find his men who had been shot down over Baghdad, while he was dealing with his own helicopter, which had been severely crippled, forcing him to land due to the extensive damage, was just another example of how he wasn't going to let life beat him. Honor and integrity are qualities that he strives hard to maintain, and he expects the same from those around him.

His good attitude and his personal religious beliefs are part of how he survives the most devastating of circumstances. His love for his comrades is commendable. He literally would give his life if it would bring even one of them back.

Deonna Laguna

PROLOGUE

I HAVE GIVEN MANY LECTURES across the United States on the events of my near-death accident. Everyone seemed so interested and wanted to know more. Many would come to me and ask if I was writing a book. I had kept a daily journal for many years on all the things I had done and really only meant my writings to be for my family. As time went on and I experienced more life-changing events, I decided to share some of these stories by publishing this book.

One of these stories is particularly difficult for me. The events of January 23, 2007, with the deaths of five of my brothers in arms, one being my sibling, made me look harder at my life. That day wasn't just about the five who lost their lives. It was a day that affected many who were involved in many different aspects of that day. This was a very hard day for many brave men who survived but have the horrible memories of losing their close friends. Survivor's guilt is a terrible thing. Unless you have experienced it, you can't understand the true extent of how it can affect you. I hope this book will help those who still suffer from it.

I have spoken with many of the brave men who were there that fateful day and many of them feel responsible in some way for what happened. They are all going through the 'what-ifs'. What if they had done this, or what if they had done that? What if they hadn't run out of ammo? To all of these brave men I would say, "There is nothing you could have done differently that would have made a difference. It was no one's fault. You all fought hard, brave and without hesitation. It is an honor for me to have worked with all of you. Remember, God is in control, not us."

<u>You Have To Live Hard To Be Hard</u> is a motto after which I have patterned my life. This is my story, growing up in conditions of extreme poverty in a small town on the outskirts of Sacramento, California called Rio Linda, and the many adventures and experiences I had after leaving home to serve my country in the United States Army.

Even after all the negative comments I received in school, mostly based on my minority background, who would have ever thought this young boy from Rio Linda would have grown up to meet with and brief a King, Ambassadors, Prime Ministers, Generals, and the President of the United States not to mention the many diplomats and VIPs across the globe. In my youth I made a promise to myself that I would show everyone that they were wrong about my family and me.

<u>You Have To Live Hard To Be Hard</u> to me means you must never give up no matter how difficult your circumstances may be. As you read this true-life story you will see how this motto has kept me from giving up when hard times have seemed unbearable. From those early days in school when I was told by adults, who I was supposed to look

up to, that I would probably flip burgers the rest of my life, to the time I spent many months in the hospital recovering from a helicopter crash that killed my best friend, and doctors telling me that my flying career had come to an end. I was also told my chances of walking normally again were not looking real good, and if I did it would not be without some kind of walking device. In reading this story, you will see the many opportunities I had to live by my motto.

I hope you will enjoy reading this book and when life seems unbearable, I hope it will inspire you in some way to apply my favorite motto, "<u>You Have To Live Hard To Be Hard</u>," which has carried me through some of the most difficult times in my life.

This book is based on my memories and the daily journals I kept over the years. There is no intention to embellish anything to make the story sound better. All the events and information about people and organizations mentioned by name in this book are not classified. This information can be found readily on the Internet. I have focused on the experiences in my life and not on the tactical procedures of the military or organizations I worked for. Conversations with certain people may not have taken place at the time or places mentioned in the book but did take place and were inserted to keep the storyline flowing. This is only a fraction of the many stories my family has heard me tell over the years. It is a true story of my life.

Dan Laguna

CHAPTER ONE
Art's Funeral

Sunlight reflected off the handles of the closed coffin. The shining box, its top covered with an American flag, lay silently beside the open grave, awaiting its final resting place. The green grass looked as if it didn't know or care that my brother was in that coffin. A few billowy clouds rolled across the blue sky, as if this were just an ordinary day. I wanted the blue sky and the clouds and the grass to somehow acknowledge the terrible grieving surrounding the coffin. Instead, the sounds of sobbing had no effect on the lovely, natural surroundings that enveloped this mournful scene.

A nearby American flag blew picture perfect in the cool breeze of that February morning near Sacramento. A steady stream of mourners was still making the ten-mile trip from the church where the memorial was held. Cars continued to arrive at the cemetery for nearly an hour. Traffic was backed up along the way as respectful drivers allowed many mourners to pass.

The fire department positioned ladder trucks along the route that draped huge American Flags above the funeral procession. A group of motorcyclists known as Patriot Guard Riders lined the route with American flags. These patriots helped to scurry away a few protestors.

My brother, Arthur Laguna, was only fifty-three years old when he was killed. He had been a Folsom Prison Guard and a Reserve Deputy Sheriff in the Sacramento area. He had served in the U.S. Army and was a helicopter pilot in the local National Guard Unit, the 229th Medevac Unit out of Mather AFB, and he also flew helicopters for the State Department security group known as Blackwater. Wearing these many uniforms, he engendered a lot of love, friendship and loyalty in many people.

Art was killed in the line of duty while he was working for Blackwater in Baghdad. I was there when he was shot down. I tried not to think of it, but the awful memories surrounding his death persistently played out in my mind. The painful image of his bloodied head in my lap, his precious life fluid wetting my fingers, refused to leave my mind.

Six young soldiers from the United States Army Honor Guard carried the coffin to the gravesite. Another young soldier held a bugle in one hand as he stood at attention. Seven other soldiers marched to a site near the grave and at the command of the officer in charge, the men fired off a twenty one-gun salute. The bugler began playing "Taps," and the mournful tune pierced the hearts of the many loved ones in attendance.

Envisioning the circumstances surrounding his death, the gunfire and the violence of that morning, was the last thing I wanted to do, but as the bugler played, it was impossible to avoid it. Unwelcome recollections of gunfire, blood and violence flashed across my memory.

Two of the soldiers slowly lifted the flag from my brother's coffin and began folding it. The sobs of my mother caught my attention and momentarily relieved me from the bloody scenes playing out in my mind. Her husband, years earlier, had been terribly wounded in combat during the Korean War in 1952, and since then she had seen two of her sons go to war. Mom was no stranger to the realities of military service. She tried to be strong as she faced her son's death, but seeing the soldiers folding the flag, and the coffin about to be placed in the ground caused her to break down.

One of the perfectly dressed soldiers carried the carefully folded flag toward my brother's widow, Mary. He waited a moment for the grieving widow to gain her composure then bowed politely as he handed her the flag that brought her once again to tears.

He said, "This flag is presented on behalf of a grateful nation and the United States Army as a token of appreciation for your loved one's honorable and faithful service."

She accepted the flag and pulled it close to her. Sobbing could be heard among loved ones in the seats behind her. At that moment, a formation of helicopters from the Sheriff Department, the National Guard, and others who had been friends of my brother flew over the cemetery in a missing man flight formation. This flight formation is typically done to pay honor to a pilot who has died in combat.

Again, ugly images flashed in my mind: the helicopter in which my brother had been shot down, bullet holes riddled through it, and broken apart from the crash landing, the bodies of my brother and three other dead men, all friends, the battle still raging around us. I secretly wished it had been me in that coffin. For a moment I stood looking at the palms of my hands remembering them covered in the blood of my brother. I wiped my hands on my pants, as if that blood was still there.

Deonna, my wife, my greatest friend, squeezed my hand. She noticed tears on my face and gave me that unspoken sign of confidence and support. She was sitting next to me while I stood for the gun salute and the bugler playing "Taps." She had been standing by my side through three decades of army life, most of it in Special Operations, which so frequently took me away from home. She, more than most, understood that soldiers cry too. She gave me children, and raised them often in my absence. On my worst days it was her support that kept me going. Neither of us spoke, but she knew my heart and knew I would have preferred to be in that coffin myself.

Even as she held tightly to my hand, I simply could not stop my mind from rehearsing the terrible details: the sound of gun fire, the smell of smoke, the explosions, the hundreds of enemy insurgents, the crashed helicopter, the desperate search for my brother, and then holding his lifeless head in my lap.

As I stood at Art's final resting place and standing within two feet of my father's headstone, my thoughts were quickly taken back to the day I was at work in the LDS hospital in Utah. I was an EMS pilot on duty when I received the call. I was told that dad was not doing very well and may not make it through the night and to come home as soon as I could. I felt a big lump forming in my throat and said I would be leaving for Sacramento within a couple of hours. We all knew Dad was terminally ill and his health was failing him fast, but in some way hoped he would get better.

Deonna and I packed quickly and headed for Sacramento, knowing the trip would take at least nine and a half hours. I continually received updates on my father's situation almost hourly and the outcome was not looking good. My family would put the phone up to my father's ear so I could talk with him every time they called. Thinking I would not be home in time I told my father that I loved him and that I was almost home. I continually said a silent prayer as I drove, asking God to allow me one more opportunity to see my father and tell him I love him in person.

When I finally arrived home, I could see how weak and frail my father was, struggling for every breath he took, I knew he did not have much time left. From the time I walked through the door, I sat there with him holding his hand until he passed away some thirty hours later. The moment he died, I kissed him on his forehead and asked him to watch over our family from heaven. I also told him not to worry that I would take care of Mom.

The nurse told us she could not understand how he hung in there so long; she thought he would have passed away two days prior. We all felt that Dad fought to stay with us until May 30th because it was his favorite day, Memorial Day.

Every Memorial Day my dad would pack up his motor home and head for Dillon's Beach on the California coast. Most of the family that could join him would.

My father was and still is my hero. I learned the true meaning of *'Live Hard To Be Hard'* from him. With all the injuries he received in combat he never once complained.

In the many weeks my mom spent day and night caring for Dad, I knew she did not have time to consider what he should wear for his funeral. The next day my brother Ricky and I went looking for the exact uniform my dad would have worn when he was in the military. After searching many Army Surplus Stores, we finally found one that had everything we needed. I was able to buy a complete uniform with all of the awards and metals that dad had earned in combat. The storeowner quickly lowered the price when he found out why I was buying such a rare uniform.

He closed the sale by saying, "Thank you for your father's service to our country."

I thanked him as we left.

Standing at Art's graveside I thought, *who would have ever guessed we would be back here at the exact location not even 3 years later?* As a family friend spoke some final words about my brother, I tried to replace the bad memories of his death with fond memories of his youth.

I remembered a moment from years earlier when Art and I were on our high school wrestling team. Art had just won a match and I walked toward him with my arms outstretched to hug him. It was a simpler time in our lives. That hug is even more meaningful to me now.

Our parents raised us on five acres just outside of Rio Linda, California. My mother calls our home "Rush Country" after the talk show host, Rush Limbaugh. He often pokes good-natured fun at the people from Rio Linda, but those years were the best of our lives.

I smiled as I remembered the old car my father gave me, and my brothers, Art and Milo. He never let us drive that car on roads, but allowed us to drive it wherever we wanted on our five acres. We learned to drive in that old car long before we were old enough to drive on the streets. I thought of the times Art was learning to drive, and how we laughed as I sat in the seat next to him.

My father was a Korean War Veteran who had been wounded by a land mine. He was a patriot whose love of our country was contagious. My brothers and I had every intention of joining the army just as soon as we were old enough.

I was told that if I volunteered for the army, I could select my first army unit. In 1972, I signed up for the army infantry and selected the 25th Infantry Division, stationed at Schofield Barracks in Hawaii. Each of my brothers came to the same army post within the next two years. For a time, we were all there together. The three of us had recently completed Sport Parachute Training, so while in Hawaii we joined an army parachute club that jumped from helicopters.

Art did his time in the regular army, then joined the National Guard unit near our home in Rio Linda, California. In 1983, he graduated from the U.S. Army Helicopter Flight School and became an army pilot. I remember the time he flew into a bad storm to rescue a woman trapped on top of her car in a flood. Art was always willing to help someone in need. Once he was even recognized by the State of California for his heroic deeds during a state emergency. Another time, as a seventeen year old, he and my mom came across a car accident. There was an injured woman frantically calling for someone to save her baby in the backseat, but no one dared go into the car because it was in flames. My mother tried to stop her teenage son, but Art ran to the burning car and saved the baby. That's the kind of guy Art was… a heart of gold, and willing to risk his life for others.

Art served as a pilot in Bosnia while in the California National Guard, often receiving hostile gunfire, and also went on dozens of drug eradication missions in California. Everyone he worked with loved him and appreciated his good-natured kindness, and his devotion to duty.

After my retirement from the U.S. Army, I was hired as Program Manager for Blackwater. At various times, I asked Art if he would like a job flying for Blackwater. Around springtime of 2006, he called and asked if the offer was still good. Art had only been home from his tour in Iraq with the National Guard a few months when he called me. He asked if I would help him get hired at Blackwater.

I smiled and said to him, "Absolutely, all you have to do is give me the word and I will put the wheels in motion."

Even though he didn't particularly like being in Iraq, Art would never be content sitting quietly at home. At the completion of each deployment, he was promptly looking for the next one or another aviation school he could attend. Art is one of the only army aviators I know who completed every aviation course available. He was a helicopter pilot, qualified in many types of helicopters, but he was also a fixed wing pilot, a maintenance test pilot, an instructor pilot, instrument flight examiner, aviation safety officer and much more. He achieved more in his shortened career than most pilots do in a lifetime. In spite of the bitter grief of the funeral, I was proud of my good brother and happy to have such fond memories of our life together.

When the graveside service ended, each of the family members walked silently past the coffin. Some dropped flowers, some dropped small handfuls of dirt, and everyone wiped away tears. As we drove away from the cemetery, I contemplated over and over again, the events of his death. I wondered what I could have done differently.

Deonna sat next to me as we slowly followed the line of cars. She reached over and placed her hand on my knee in an attempt to console me. She knew what I was pondering, even without my saying so. I drifted away and relived every moment of that ugly day that had occurred only a week earlier.

CHAPTER TWO
Little Bird Down

JANUARY 23, 2007 STARTED LIKE every other day. Each morning, at 5:30, Art and I would meet outside by our hangar so we could begin our walk to the Palace Gym together for our early morning workout. While we were walking, we would always find ourselves talking about our families back home, wondering what they were doing and hoping all was well with them. Talking about our families helped us both forget about where we were for a short time. It felt so good to laugh, joke and talk about the old times, something I have not been able to do for a long time with my brother. The time we spent together was very special to me because it gave us the opportunity to catch up since our former careers had taken us both in different directions for the past thirty-four years. I now wish those walks had taken us at least thirty minutes and not the ten minutes it had, so I could have spent more time with my brother.

The evening before the deaths of my brother Art and four other good friends, we had received our mission briefings and it was my job to make the assignments. I received intelligence reports on the weather, the enemy threats, and the mission for the following day. I organized the flight teams that would fly escort over the convoy for VIPs, typically State Department personnel. We coordinated our air security efforts with the ground convoy and every detail of the trip was carefully considered.

On this morning I assigned Kevin McLemore to serve as the Flight Lead with Bob Rogers as his co-pilot, and my brother Art with Ron Johnson as their wingman. Each had a crew of four, consisting of a pilot, co-pilot and two door gunners. The Flight Lead was given the call sign Blackwater 3-3, and Art was known as Blackwater 3-4. The wingman flew behind the lead and was there to protect the lead crew as necessary.

Blackwater, now known as Xe Services LLC, is made up of former military specialists, mostly Green Berets, Rangers, Air Force Para Rescue, Navy SEALS and U.S. Marines. We were hired by Blackwater in support of the U.S. State Department to provide security for diplomats in war zones. We worked side by side with the military units and served our country with the same dedication as we had when we were in the military.

Occasionally you hear a news story about Blackwater security teams being overly aggressive in defending the VIPs they escort through high-risk areas. To this day, not one of our VIPs has been injured. The truth is that Blackwater Personal Security Detachments are highly trained, hand selected, and very experienced in what they do. They are professionals who only fire their weapons when there is a significant risk to the VIPs they provide security for. Blackwater Personal Security Detachments have performed thousands of escort missions for State Department and other VIP personnel around the world and have fired their weapons only when their lives or the lives of the diplomat that they were protecting was threatened. These security teams have a very strict set of Rules Of Engagement (ROE) they live by.

Many news reports paint a picture of Blackwater Personal Security Detachments as a bunch of rogue, trigger-happy guns for hire, and killing for the thrill of it. Nothing is further from the truth. The real bad guys in Iraq are the ones who intentionally kill thousands of innocent people with random explosions and who use butcher knives to carve off the heads of decent men and women who dare to hope for a better life. Those murderous thugs are the reason Blackwater exists.

Employees of Blackwater work directly for the State Department of the U.S. Government. We often work side-by-side with the U. S. military units to protect the diplomatic processes in Iraq. Our mission is to serve the good people of Iraq who are working to bring peace to their country. Blackwater employees feel that their efforts and sacrifices are for the same causes they fought for when they were wearing military uniforms.

Before I became a Program Manager for Blackwater Aviation, I had retired as a former Green Beret and a Special Operations Aviator assigned to 160th SOAR, known as the TF160 (Night Stalkers). We are known as Night Stalkers because our training and missions are done after dark. I had 30 years of service in the United States Army, serving most of that time in Special Operations. My years in Special Operations provided me a world of experience in counter terrorism and Special Operations missions.

I am a religious man and I have a strong faith in God and have often felt prompted to take certain actions, not always knowing why but feeling confident it was the right thing to do. My work with

Blackwater in Iraq allowed me to take thirty days of vacation every few months. However, in December of 2006, I felt I needed to get back to Iraq early, so I didn't take my entire vacation time. My loving yet disappointed wife gave me her full support.

Upon my arrival in Baghdad, it was clear that the Red Zone was unusually tense. In Baghdad there are two areas, the Red Zone and the Green Zone. The Green Zone is an area that is marked by the well-known T-walls. T-walls are slabs of concrete approximately twelve feet tall, five feet wide, two feet thick, with a wide base to stand erect. There are hundreds of thousand of these concrete walls surrounding places like the U.S. Embassy and compounds where American and coalition forces live.

The air in Baghdad is always polluted and smoke-filled from oil refineries and bombings, but something else was in the air that fateful day, something foreboding and sinister. The next few weeks were spent performing typical missions, but we were particularly careful in everything we did. Intelligence reports indicated that insurgent activity was on the rise and the attack threat was increasing.

On this dreadful day, January 23rd, 2007, our mission was to escort a diplomat from the Iraq Reconstruction Management Office at the U.S. Embassy to the Iraq Public Works Annex. The annex is in the oldest part of Baghdad, east of the Tigris River. Missions like this one are routine, and except for the tense feelings in my heart, nothing was out of the ordinary. Though flights to the Public Works Annex are routine, the area surrounding the annex had become a hotbed of insurgents who had vowed to shoot down a helicopter, preferably a Blackwater helicopter. Intelligence reports indicated the insurgents had placed a bounty on Blackwater personnel, so we paid close attention to the insurgent activity around the Public Works Annex.

A couple of years earlier, four Blackwater Contractors were

ambushed in Fallujah. The bodies were mutilated, set afire and left hanging from a bridge. The insurgents had frequent opportunity to hit Blackwater teams. Our jobs put us in the air and on the streets all day, every day. Before the day Art was shot down at least twenty-two other Blackwater Contractors had been killed.

Even though Art was my brother, I didn't show favoritism toward him. He was given difficult missions just like the other pilots and crew. Our flight headquarters was located at LZ Washington, next to the U.S. Baghdad Embassy in the Green Zone. Each morning the pilots and crewmembers assembled and prepared all their mission equipment before they attended the morning briefing.

By 7:30 that morning the crews were on the flight line. They performed these missions every day, always memorizing the routes to and from the destination. Preparation for one of these missions, even though they were an everyday occurrence, was a serious matter. We frequently received gunfire from the insurgents but would seldom fire back, because the insurgents would pop out of a window, fire on us, and then retreat. Blackwater rules of engagement did not allow us to fire on a location unless we could positively identify those who were shooting at us.

Because we always expect to take enemy fire, the preflight inspections are a time for careful preparations, as well as somber reflection. The door gunners would take time to place additional body armor on the helicopter floors and seats for extra protection. The Little Bird helicopters did not have the same built-in protection as the U.S. Army helicopters, so the door gunners developed this homespun method of protecting themselves from small arms fire.

As we worked that morning, we heard the ominous sounds of explosions in distant parts of the city, and we hoped that one of our convoys had not been attacked by insurgents. At first, nobody said anything as the explosions rang out. We'd all been in similar circumstances and could envision what was going on.

Art broke the silence. "I wonder who got hit? Hope it wasn't any friendlies."

Kevin McLemore, the Lead Pilot for this mission, called out to the door gunners, "Hey guys, keep an eye out. If you see the location of those explosions, let me know. I want to know if it was coalition forces that got hit."

If coalition forces were under attack, Kevin and Art's helicopters would have completed their mission and then flown directly to the scene of the ambush to offer air support.

It takes a special breed of man to be a door gunner. They have all been in combat and have the kind of experience required for our missions. The gunners sit in the open doors of the helicopter, and with nerves of steel, they do their jobs fully exposed to enemy gunfire.

Attached to the helicopter by a one-inch wide strap or rope, they are expected to seek out hostile threats and engage targets with precision rifle fire from a fast-moving unstable platform that's yanking and banking like a rollercoaster while in the hands of their pilots in the front seats. They fly at around a hundred miles per hour, at treetop level, between buildings and trees, all the while placing accurate sniper gunfire as the pilots do wild maneuvers that would get them grounded for life in the civilian or military world. If you asked a door gunner, he'd tell you he has the coolest job on the planet.

Art prepared his helicopter and had a few words with his crew. His guys worked together closely, putting their lives on the line every day, so they became more than simply coworkers; they were brothers. They live together, train together, laugh together, and on this morning they would die together.

As their boss, I carried a Motorola 5000 radio with an earpiece so

I could monitor all the radio chatter between the crews. As the flight crews made their final preparations, I walked back to my office. With one final look back at the crews, I waved to Art. This was something I always did before Art left on his mission, just to say "good luck brother."

After they completed their engine run-up and communication checks, the Little Birds lifted off to perform a reconnaissance of the route for the ground convoy. The diplomats usually traveled on the ground in a four-vehicle convoy to and from their meetings. The ground convoy for this mission was code named "Raven 7," a Blackwater Protective Security Detail (PSD), also made up of mostly former Special Operations guys.

When Blackwater 3-3 and 3-4 completed the route reconnaissance, the updated information was given to the convoy commander of Raven 7, and the mission began. The ground convoy then maneuvered through the Green Zone, out the security gate, and into the Red Zone.

As Raven 7 entered the Red Zone on the planned route, Blackwater 3-3 and 3-4 were overhead in an orbit. One Little Bird would stay at least a half-mile ahead of the convoy and make changes to the route based on information they gathered in their ongoing reconnaissance flight. If they sensed any insurgent activity or a person on a roof, or spotted someone with a weapon, they would advise a route change for Raven 7.

Both helicopter crews constantly examined the route and the convoy. They had been briefed on the exact make up of the convoy, so they could identify which vehicles were part of the ground team and could identify any vehicle that should not be traveling with the convoy.

In my office at LZ (Landing Zone) Washington, I monitored the radio chatter to keep abreast of the mission. Everything went well, and the VIP with Raven 7 was safely delivered to the Public Works Annex. The pilots then began their short flight back to the LZ, but just as they approached LZ Washington, things began to go bad.

Minutes after both helicopters had landed back at LZ Washington, I was in my office doing paperwork when I received a phone call from the Tactical Operations Center (TOC).

They said a ground team was receiving hostile fire and wanted us to go assist them by breaking contact with the insurgents and escorting them back into the Green Zone.

I said, *"Roger that . . . they are on their way."* I quickly ran out the door because in this business every second counts; it literally could mean life or death for one of our Blackwater brothers.

As the Quick Reaction Force (QRF) for all teams, the Little Bird crews are never far from their helicopter and are always ready when a call requesting help comes in.

I quickly located Kevin McLemore (Blackwater 3-3), briefed him on the team in contact, and advised him to check in with the TOC (Tactical Operations Center) for more details once his team was airborne.

In less than two minutes, Blackwater 3-3 and 3-4 were airborne and headed in the direction of the ground team that was in contact and needed their help.

I returned to my office to continue my work, with the volume up on my Motorola 5000 radio so I could monitor the communication between the Little Birds and the team in contact. After they helped the ground team break contact and get back into the Green Zone safely, Blackwater 3-3 and 3-4 were back on the ground at LZ Washington.

Minutes after Blackwater 3-3 and 3-4 were back, I received

another phone call stating that the ground team (Raven 7) we had escorted to the Public Works Annex earlier was receiving sporadic small-arms fire. They also observed a couple of Iraqis on a rooftop close to their venue, with what appeared to be a Rocket Propelled Grenade Launcher (RPG).

Again, I immediately briefed Kevin McLemore (Blackwater 3-3) on Raven 7's situation. The Little Bird Lead Pilot gave his crew a hasty briefing and quickly took-off to see what kind of help they could offer Raven 7 at the Public Works Annex.

The two helicopters arrived at the Public Works Annex in less than three minutes. Raven 7 was still receiving hostile fire. The TOC often called on us to help with air support under conditions like this.

Typically, the plan was to fly immediately to the ambush site, provide enough firepower to help the convoy disengage, then escort them back into the Green Zone.

As soon as Blackwater 3-3 and 3-4 arrived over the Public Works Annex they came under very heavy volumes of ground fire from both heavy and light weapons. We later learned that nearly a thousand insurgents had gathered for this well-organized attack. Over the next couple of hours, the insurgents would fire from rooftops, out of windows, and from trucks and cars.

Within a few seconds after the lead helicopter, Blackwater 3-3 arrived on the scene, the left door gunner, Steve Gernet, was hit by sniper fire.

Kevin hollered, "G-man's hit . . . he's falling out. I'm gonna set down and help him."

G-Man is a nickname for Steve Gernet, a no-nonsense, retired Green Beret and the left-side door gunner on Blackwater 3-3.

After he landed on the roof of a nearby building, Kevin jumped out of the helicopter leaving the Little Bird running with his copilot Bob Rogers at the controls. The right door gunner, Paul Mendoza also jumped out and they both ran to the aid of G-Man. It was too late to help him. A single large caliber bullet had hit him in the head and killed him instantly. The tether and harness he was wearing kept him from falling to the ground.

I heard Kevin McLemore radio to the TOC, "We have a casualty and are heading to the CSH (pronounced cash) pad."

The CSH pad is a landing pad at the Combat Support Hospital in the Green Zone. Over my radio, I heard other radio chatter among the crew.

"3-3 . . . what's your status!" I shouted as they were making their approach.

Kevin responded with a very somber tone, "We're headed for the CSH Pad."

"Roger that . . . I'll meet you there."

McLemore didn't tell me G-man was dead, but I could sense it was bad. Nobody spoke over the radio for the next few minutes.

I ran to the hangar to round up another crew. I grabbed Frank Paul (Cyrus), Mark Caracci and Emmett Rose and got another helicopter ready to go. Within five minutes we were airborne and on our way to the CSH pad.

I radioed Kevin, "3-3 . . . this is 3-5."

"3-5 . . . this is 3-3 . . . we're short final at the CSH pad." His voice was sullen.

"Roger, I'll cap you." (Orbit overhead)

I flew overhead security for the couple of minutes it took to escort the body of our brother, G-Man, to the hospital. The other door gunner, Steve Cathey stayed at the hospital with G-Man. All three helicopters then flew back to LZ Washington. As we flew, no words were spoken, but I continued to monitor the chatter that took place between Raven 7 and the TOC about the ongoing firefight.

While I sat in my helicopter waiting for the rotor blades to come to a stop after shutdown, I could see the look of anguish and despair on each crewmember's face. Up until now Blackwater Aviation had never lost anyone in combat, and we had been in many firefights in the three-plus years we had been operating in Baghdad.

We were on the ground for only a few minutes. During that time, a couple of Blackwater personnel pulled a water hose over to the helicopter and began washing the blood from the floor of Blackwater 3-3. A helmet, full of gore from the head wound was on the ground, with the label 'G-Man' taped to the back. Nobody wanted to look at it or pick it up, but the guy with the hose finally picked it up and washed it out. Though the extent of damage to Kevin's helicopter at this time was unknown, I thought his radio was damaged by the gunfire. With the possibility of bullet holes in the helicopter, I didn't want him flying until the maintenance guys could check it out.

I walked up to Kevin who stood facing me, not wanting to say much. The entire left side of his uniform was covered with the blood of his friend. There was a look of sorrow on all of our faces, but there were no feelings of anger or vengeance. We were all professionals who had been in many firefights, and we knew the risks involved. They stood there awaiting my orders.

A dozen of my guys from Blackwater Aviation had heard about the shooting and were all gathered at the flight line, and they all volunteered to join us on the next flight. Although many volunteered to go, I kept Mark Caracci and Emmett Rose as my door gunners.

Minutes after being on the ground, I received a call from the TOC that Raven 7 was still under fire and needed our help ASAP.

I said, "Roger that . . . we're on our way."

As Cyrus started up the helicopter, I noticed Shane Stanfield, nicknamed War Baby, jumping into our helicopter as door gunner. Art and I looked similar and I suppose he thought I was Art.

"War Baby, wrong bird!"

He looked at me, smiled, and ran to Art's bird. It was the last time I saw him alive. War Baby is a nickname given to the youngest guy in the unit. Shane was only twenty-two when we hired him at Blackwater and twenty-five when his life was taken.

War Baby headed for Art's bird just as my gunners arrived and strapped in.

I hollered, "Kevin, you stay here and get your bird checked out before flying, and make sure they fix your radio. Art, you fly wing for me and we'll get back to Raven 7. Let's go! Let's go! We gotta get back out there!"

My shouts breathed new vigor into the crewmembers and we all jumped back into action. I asked my co-pilot, Cyrus, to take the controls so I could have a better opportunity to observe and assess the situation on the ground. His real name was Frank Paul. He was a hard chargin' guy who had gotten his nickname from a character in the movie *Con Air*. Most of the guys didn't even know Cyrus's real name.

Blackwater 3-3 stayed on the ground while Ron Johnson and Art in 3-4 and Cyrus and I in 3-5 lifted off to go to the aid of our brothers in need. Radio chatter made it clear that more and more insurgents were joining the attack.

As we arrived back at the Public Works Annex, the situation was very hot. Hundreds of insurgents were involved in the attacks; some were on roofs, others were in the streets, and all were firing on Raven 7 as well as the army units who had responded to the attacks. More army units, including a Stryker Company showed up. Everyone loved seeing Stryker vehicles because they have a great reputation as a hard-fighting, quick-reaction force. They were pouring onto the scene in an attempt to rescue Raven 7.

During my career I have seen plenty of enemy fire, but this day was unlike any other firefight. The volume of gunfire and Rocket-Propelled Grenades (RPGs) was astounding. Later intelligence reports estimated there were close to a thousand insurgents shooting at us, which would explain the heavy volumes of gunfire.

Our Blackwater ground units were fighting it out side-by-side with the Army Stryker guys. We flew at a very low altitude, as low as a hundred feet off the ground. This was the only way to get a visual contact with the enemy and identify their locations. From any higher altitude, our door gunners were not as effective. We constantly performed evasive maneuvers as we were fired upon. Art was flying wing for me and was only seventy-five feet behind me.

After less than a minute flying over Raven 7, I heard my brother over the radio yelling, "I'm hit! I'm hit! I'm going back!"

Cyrus wheeled the Little Bird around, and in seconds we were turned around looking for Art; but he was gone. We quickly scanned the sky looking for them, but didn't see them.

"3-4 . . . this is 3-5 . . . where are you?"

I called him over and over, my voice growing frantic. We hoped they headed back toward the Green Zone but were unable to contact us because their radio might have been shot up.

"3-4 . . . this is 3-5 . . . if you can't talk, just click your radio." Nothing.

We started a systematic search starting at the Public Works Annex and working outward, Cyrus sailing through the air, street after street.

"3-4 . . . this is 3-5." Still nothing.

I called the TOC, "We have a Little Bird down and have no coms with them . . . do you know anything?"

"We have no word on a downed helicopter."

The TOC was monitoring and coordinating the events of the battle.

"3-4 . . . this is 3-5 . . . Cat Daddy, Art, where are you?"

Cat Daddy was a nickname for Ron Johnson, the daring young Lead Pilot with Art, but he gave no radio response.

I hoped that they were still alive and were unable to respond only due to a damaged radio, but deep down inside I knew something was very wrong. Art and his crew were shot down somewhere in the middle of the insurgent attack. We frantically searched up and down the streets. The enemy gunfire was very intense, but my door gunners did their job like heroes as we flew through the gunfire searching for our downed brothers.

"3-4 . . . this is 3-5 . . . Cat Daddy, Art, where are you?" No response.

My blood ran cold. Each of the crew carried around 120 rounds of ammunition with their personal weapons. That wouldn't last long in a ground fight as intense as this one. Flying dangerously low, our Little Bird helicopter was being hit by automatic rifle fire, as well as large caliber machine gun fire. Bullets rattled through the bird, damaging some of our electronics. I silently prayed for protection of my men, even as we flew through a hail of bullets.

I glanced around to see both door gunners, hoping they had not been wounded. Both gunners were hanging in the doors carefully scanning the ground for our missing crew. They learned to steel themselves against the fear of incoming bullets and keep their heads cool while they were fighting back. Ours was a fierce way of life.

Over and over I called the downed bird. "3-4 . . . this is 3-5 . . . Cat Daddy, Art, where are you?" Still nothing.

We continued our restless search for the missing Little Bird in a life-and-death struggle to find them. I imagined my brother and friends being captured and what the awful consequences might be. I wondered what they were going through at that very minute, and the thought was terrifying. I hated to think of it, but I knew they were better off dead than captured.

I continuously contacted the TOC. "We have a Little Bird down . . . do you have any reports on the location?"

The TOC was getting some conflicting information in the heat of the battle and gave me various locations to check, but they kept giving me latitude and longitude coordinates. That was a typical format for searching, but in this case, our GPS unit had been hit by gunfire and was useless. I could not use latitude and longitude. A dozen times I went through the same dialogue with the TOC.

I would say, "Don't give me latitude and longitude coordinates, my GPS is shot up. Give me a direction and distance from a known crossroad or building!"

But repeatedly, the TOC radio operator only gave me useless coordinates. I placed a radio call to Blackwater Air Asset Coordinator, John Hayes.

"This is Blackwater 3-5 . . . we need every available air crew to join in this search."

Hayes was monitoring the action and was already working on it. "Roger that 3-5, we have other help on the way, including a UAV."

Hayes coordinated with the army for an Unmanned Aerial Vehicle (UAV) to fly up and down the streets looking for Art and his crew. Later in the battle, it was the UAV that first spotted the downed bird, but the crew was not visible. Gunfire continuously pounded our bird, and still the gunners remained unhurt. Each time I checked on the gunners. I thanked God for keeping them safe.

Down on the ground the Raven 7 guys were fighting for their lives. Continuous radio chatter often included the familiar voices of friends on the ground teams. "3-4 . . . this is 3-5 . . . try clicking your radio! Cat Daddy, Art, where are you." Still nothing. "Art . . . say something if you can!" Still no response.

We all hoped they were alive and working on an escape and evasion plan. At one point we were flying low, checking out an area where the missing crew may have crash-landed when we were hit very hard by heavy caliber machine gun fire. The whole helicopter vibrated as the large caliber rounds busted through the bird. We were so close to an insurgent heavy machine gun that we could hear and feel the percussion of the gun above the noise of the helicopter.

Unfortunately, we could not see the machine gun. We discovered later that the gun, a DShK Soviet 12.7mm (50 caliber) heavy machine gun had been placed in the back of a large civilian-style truck with a canopy. The insurgents would pull the cover open and fire on us and then pull the cover back so we could not see them. They knew that our rules of engagement forbade us from firing unless we could actually see them, and they used those rules against us.

Just as that heavy machine gun rattled our helicopter, the situation nearly turned much worse. Two insurgents on a rooftop behind us, out of view of our door gunners, stood up to fire an RPG at us. From their angle, they would likely have shot us down except for the fact that both insurgents were quickly killed by an alert Blackwater DDM (Designated Defense Marksman) sniper only seconds before they would have shot us down. Immediately another insurgent picked up the same RPG and the Blackwater DDM, with the same quickness and accuracy, killed the insurgent, making it the third time we were saved by our sniper.

The DDM, Patrick Johnston, and his spotter, Jeff Wright, were part of a Blackwater low profile team. These were special teams that drove ordinary civilian vehicles and blended in with the population so they didn't draw any attention to themselves. They had moved into position on the roof of the Public Works Annex when the attack took place, and their quick action saved our lives.

Every available asset from Blackwater and the army was moving into the area to join the counter attack against the insurgents. We had four Blackwater helicopters involved in the search. The radio chatter was nearly constant from all the different units involved in the fight. Each time the radio was keyed rattling gunfire could be heard in the background.

I tried to keep a professional demeanor, but I noticed my voice was showing some desperation. I called again, "3-3 . . . this is 3-5 . . . Cat Daddy . . . if you can hear me, but can't talk, just key your radio." Still nothing.

We continued flying through the firefight with bullet holes throughout the aircraft but without injury to the crew. One of the bullets hit the bird only a few inches from my head. I thanked God for His protecting hand.

After about twenty minutes of searching, the helicopter was so punctured with bullet holes it was vibrating badly and not flying well. I wanted to keep searching for my brother and his crew, but I had another crew to think of.

Just then Cyrus hollered out, "The helicopter is in trouble. We're going down."

We were just hit with a large caliber machine gun again; you could feel the rounds rip through the rotor blades.

It felt as though the helicopter was coming apart right in midair. A short distance from us was an open field at the Iraq Ministry of Health, a site where I had landed before while I was escorting VIPs. Cyrus did an amazing job of nursing our badly damaged Little Bird to the open field. We didn't have much choice in the matter, because the bird was going down with or without a clear landing site. We hoped the area would be relatively safe but were disappointed to discover otherwise.

I called the TOC. "This is Blackwater 3-5. We are landing at the Ministry of Health, and the bird is too damaged to fly. We need every available army unit to help find our missing bird."

The TOC was already on top of the situation. "Roger that, Blackwater 3-5 . . . we have Apache and Blackhawk helicopters joining the search . . . give me your status . . . do you have any casualties?"

"We have no casualties. Just get me the location of the downed Little Bird . . . remember, my GPS is shot up, I need a reference from a building or a bridge!"

As we were making our forced landing to the Ministry of Health, Raven 24 was alerted to move to Raven 7's location to assist them in getting the diplomat and Raven 7's team back into the Green Zone.

Raven 24, Chuck Person's Counter Assault Team, immediately departed from FOB Shields (Forward operating Base) and began fighting their way through streets and alleys to the Public Works Annex to assist Raven 7. As soon as they arrived at Raven 7's location they received a call that two Little Birds were down in the city. They immediately departed the Public Works Annex to begin the search for the downed Little Birds. Raven 26 now picked up the mission to assist Raven 7 and they had to fight their way to the Public Works Annex in order to assist Raven 7. When they arrived at Raven 7's location, they immediately loaded the diplomat into their vehicle. With Raven 7's convoy mixed in with Raven 26's convoy they fought their way back to the Green Zone. The diplomat was safely returned to the U.S. Embassy and Raven 26 prepared to return into the Red Zone to help with the search for the downed Little Birds.

Meanwhile, Cyrus carefully landed our helicopter and then shut the bird down, turning off all the power. I quickly jumped out of the helicopter to assess the damage. The door gunners also jumped out and assumed security positions. As the rotor blades slowed to a stop, I could see that three of our five blades, as well as the fuselage, were riddled with bullet holes. One rotor blade had a hole as big as my fist. The damage was worse than I thought, but the situation was about to get much worse.

My attention was diverted to the east where I could see dozens, maybe a hundred or more insurgents gathering. The insurgents saw us land and within a couple of minutes there were dozens of enemy fighters racing toward us. I noticed several Iraqi policemen standing on the roof of the Ministry of Health building, and I was frustrated to see the Iraqi policemen, who were supposed to be on our side, pointing out our position to the insurgents. I knew we didn't have much time. There was no way the four of us could defend our position. If we stayed there, we would certainly be killed.

Our best option seemed to be starting up the damaged helicopter in an attempt to clear the surrounding buildings and fly the hundred or so yards to the Tigris River, and then travel along the river back to LZ Washington. Even if we crash-landed en route, we couldn't be in a worse situation than what we were already facing.

As the three of us jumped back into the helicopter, I shouted, "Cyrus, crank it up and let's get out of here!"

The helicopter shuddered as it cranked up. I didn't think we would even get off the ground, let alone clear the buildings. Cyrus nursed the bird off the ground and struggled to gain altitude, but we managed to get over the rooftops with no room to spare. We then descended to just above the water level of the Tigris River.

Not believing the bird could fly much longer, we prepared for a crash landing in the river. If we crashed, we had no one to help us and would likely have been hurt, perhaps drowned. I prayed again for the safety of our crew and hoped for a miracle.

Just as we cleared the buildings, Kevin McLemore in Blackwater 3-3 contacted me. "3-5 . . . this is 3-3 . . . I'm right behind you."

Kevin had made the necessary repairs to his bird and to the radio and was monitoring my latest conversation with the TOC. He knew we had landed at the Ministry of Health but could not contact us because our radio was off while we powered down to inspect the helicopter damage. Hearing that we had another crew flying behind us was a huge relief. If we did crash, we would have immediate help.

Now that we had a wing to provide security if we crash-landed, we breathed a little easier. In fact, as we reached the relative safety of the river, I realized I had been holding my breath since we had left the Ministry of Health. I exhaled loudly and thanked God we had escaped death yet again.

"3-3 . . . this is 3-5 . . . glad you are with us brother . . . we're headed to LZ Washington."

Kevin could see the shuddering of our helicopter. "3-5 . . . that bird don't look so good."

We didn't respond because the situation was too tense to speak. As we flew down the river, I called over the radio to our maintenance crew on the flight line. "I need three main rotor blades replaced immediately! We'll be landing in two minutes."

I never received a response but when we arrived the maintenance guys were ready for us. Three minutes after leaving the Ministry of Health, we were back to LZ Washington at the Blackwater hangar. The moment the skids touched ground, Cyrus shut the helicopter down and the maintenance crews went to work with three new blades. Four mechanics came out and stared in amazement for a few seconds as they saw how damaged the bird was. Then the swarm of mechanics performed like a perfectly choreographed NASCAR Speedway pit crew. They later said that it was a miracle that the helicopter would even fly at all, let alone land safely twice. Miracle was the right word.

While the mechanics anxiously worked on my helicopter, I made radio contact with another Blackwater helicopter crew that had joined us in the search. None of them had yet found the missing crew, and all of them were taking the same machinegun fire that had shot us down. The incessant sounds of the battle, only a short distance away, continued while our bird was being repaired. Smoke and dust drifted into the sky, and we silently hoped our friends were still alive.

Less than ten minutes after we had landed, we were back in the helicopter getting ready to lift off again. Normally, the mechanics would take the time to balance the rotors, but we didn't have time for that. We had a missing crew shot down in enemy-held streets, and we were desperate to continue the search.

During the work on the rotor blades, the group grew much larger at the Blackwater hangar. By now everyone had heard of the two Little Birds that had gone down. They all began collecting their gear and weapons volunteering to help in the search. From the flight line we could hear the gunfire and explosions of the fighting, and each of these men knew the danger, however all were willing and anxious to help.

A gunner named Paul Perkerson, known as Elvis because of his long sideburns, knew I needed two gunners because my current two gunners, Mark and Emmet, were needed to help coordinate the ground-search effort. He slapped the guy next to him, Mark "Doc" York, a former Green Beret Medic and the two of them ran toward my bird. We already had one man dead, a helicopter shot down and a raging firefight going on only a few minutes east of us, but our gunners didn't show a second of hesitation.

As both helicopters left the compound, I radioed again for Art. "3-3 . . . this is 3-5."

It was no surprise to get no response, but I was compelled to keep trying, hoping to hear his voice. The army used an electronic device to interrupt the triggering mechanism for Improvised Explosive Devices (IEDs). Unfortunately, the device also interfered with our radio transmissions. Blackwater helicopters, unlike the army's, could not compensate for the interference, so our radio systems became nearly useless over the next twenty minutes.

Cyrus continued flying a methodical route up and down streets as we desperately tried to find the missing crew. The battle raged on the ground and we continually took gunshots through the bird. Every time I checked on the crew, they were miraculously unharmed.

Because of the interruptions to the radio caused by electronic jamming devices from the military vehicles, we did not know that one of the U.S. Army helicopters had been flying over the crash site and that an Army Stryker vehicle was on the way.

The Stryker guys fought their way to the downed helicopter hoping to rescue the crew, but as they arrived on the scene they saw insurgents dragging the bodies away from the crash site. The Stryker crew engaged the insurgents and then hustled over to the four bodies and dragged them back to the side of their vehicle. The dead bodies of our friends had been dragged from the crashed helicopter and then shot in the head by the insurgents. The four brave men died when their helicopter crashed, but it was a common occurrence for the insurgents to mutilate the bodies of their enemies. That was why I was so determined to find my guys before the insurgents did. The Stryker personnel with one Blackwater ground team remained on the scene to secure the helicopter, and they placed the bodies of our friends in body bags.

Unaware that the army had already found the crash site, we continued our search. When we noticed some soldiers on the ground, my door gunner tapped me on the shoulder and pointed them out, near the Public Works Annex.

There was a small clearing next to them, and because we were not getting any radio information, I said to Cyrus, "Put us down over there . . . maybe we can get some info from him."

Cyrus landed next to the soldier and Elvis, the left-side door gunner, disconnected and jumped out before we completely landed. After a few seconds with the soldier, Elvis jumped back in and connected his harness.

He shouted over all the noise. "He doesn't know anything about the Little Bird, but he said there were four bodies up the road near a Stryker vehicle."

Elvis pointed in the direction of the Stryker vehicle and Cyrus quickly lifted off. It took us only a minute to find the Stryker crew and the crash site. The helicopter was terribly damaged from a hard crash landing. From the air it was clear that the tail boom was completely separated from the main fuselage and the rotor blades were bent upward. The nose of the helicopter was completely destroyed. I had every reason to believe my brother and friends were dead. Still, I needed to see those bodies to confirm what I suspected.

Next to the Stryker vehicle were five army soldiers defending the site where the bodies of our comrades were zipped in body bags. The battle was still raging around them, but they stayed on site and did their jobs. Uncommon valor was common on that morning. One of our Blackwater ground teams had already made their way to the crash site and they were fighting alongside the army guys, helping to secure the crash site against the insurgents who desperately wanted the wreckage and the bodies.

I had always told my guys that I would never leave them behind no matter what happened. We each felt the same way, so there was no question as to what needed to be done. About a hundred yards from the crash site was a clearing in the street wide enough to land the helicopter.

"Cyrus, put me down in that spot right there and then fly back to LZ Washington. I'll make my own way back."

I pointed to the spot in the street where we had received heavy volumes of automatic fire just minutes before, but it was the only place clear enough to land, even though it was surrounded by insurgents. Although it was risky to make the landing, Cyrus flew straight to the landing site and set the bird down. I jumped out and again directed Cyrus to go back to the Green Zone with the rest of the flight crew, which was against standard procedure. It was typical for the gunners to be dropped off and the pilots to fly the bird to a safe location while the gunners did the reconnaissance mission to find and identify the bodies. But this was a little bit different; my brother was out there and I wanted to be the one to identify him and the others.

Cyrus looked boldly in my eyes and said, "I ain't goin' nowhere, boss. You go do what you gotta do, and we're waitin' right here for ya."

I was proud of them and impressed with their courage and loyalty.

We all knew the danger of parking our crew right in the middle of the battle, but we all understood how important it was to identify the bodies. A lot of intense fighting was going on, and the bodies may not have been our guys. However in spite of the danger, I had to make sure.

Again, I told Cyrus to take the crew and bird back to LZ Washington. Again, he refused to leave me. There was not much time for debate. As I jumped out of the helicopter, I took a deep breath, thinking this could be my last day on Earth. As I left my friends at the helicopter and started what seemed to be the final walk of my life, I can remember seeing a quick flash of Deonna's beautiful face appearing before me as if she was telling me like she always does, "I love you."

Elvis disconnected himself from the harness and shouted, "You're not doin' this alone, boss. I'll be right behind ya."

The sound of his voice brought me back to the task at hand, which was to find and identify my guys. Cyrus and Doc York stayed at the helicopter, a potential prize for insurgents who were on all the surrounding rooftops. In hindsight, it was a really bad idea to place the crew and bird in that kind of danger. We're all lucky to have survived that decision.

It's hard to describe the emotions of the moment: apprehension at the thought of identifying the bodies; fear of making a widow of my wife, and the wives of my crew; pride in the courage and fortitude of these brave men refusing to leave me even when I ordered them to fly to safety; and fierce determination to accomplish the awful task in front of us. But there was no time to hug these brave men. Instead, I took off down the street. We had a hundred yards to run through the insurgent's gunfire to get to the Stryker crew. With weapons at our shoulders, constantly on the lookout for someone shooting at us, we made our way down the narrow street.

Tommy Vargas, who was part of a Quick Reaction Force (QRF) responding to the downed helicopter search, later told me they were in some intense fighting when he noticed my Little Bird landing in the intersection down the street. He initially thought it was crash landing, because he didn't believe anybody would dare land in the middle of the fighting. He and his buddies began pouring intense gunfire at the insurgents along the street to cover us as we ran up the street. If that man had not been so alert, we may have walked into our own deaths. I considered it another miracle that we survived our run down that dangerous Baghdad Street.

When I arrived at the relative safety of the Stryker vehicle, I went straight to the four body bags. The army crew knew we were there to find the bodies of our friends. I knelt at the first body bag and unzipped it with a lump in my throat. For a moment, I could hear no gunfire, no explosions, and no sounds of war. For me, everything was silent as I unzipped the first body bag and saw the face of Lead Pilot Ron Johnson. Cat Daddy and I had been friends for years. We had been in the same Special Operations unit years earlier in the army. Then I knew that the other three body bags would contain the bodies of my other friends and my brother, Arthur Laguna.

As I slowly unzipped that second body bag, my heart was beating so hard I thought it was going to tear right through my chest; my breathing was so fast I was at a point of hyperventilation and before I knew it, I was staring right into Art's face. At that moment it felt as if all the blood ran right out of my body and my eyes began to fill with tears. Tears trickled down my face as I whispered, "I'm sorry. I'm sorry. I love you, Art. Please forgive me."

I gently laid my brother's head down and zipped up his body

bag. I felt responsible for his death and honestly wished I could trade places with him. As I identified the first two bodies, Elvis unzipped the other two bags and confirmed that they were our other friends, Casey Cassavant and Shane Stanfield (War Baby). We identified the bodies and there was nothing more we could do.

Elvis must have thought we were on the ground at that location too long, because he said, *"Let's go, boss"* a few times before I actually recognized his voice.

I acknowledged him and said, "Roger that. Let's go." But all I wanted to do was sit there and hold my brother. With my brother's head in my lap I bent down and kissed him on the forehead, again saying, "I'm sorry. I love you."

I walked over to the Stryker vehicle commander, an Army Major, and asked him, "Can you make sure my guys in the body bags get back to the Green Zone?"

He glanced down and saw the blood on my hands and clothes from holding my brother's head, and replied, "I promise you we will get them out of here."

The brave men in that Stryker unit had placed themselves right in the middle of the firefight, surrounded, in order to find the crashed helicopter and protect the bodies of men they didn't even know. I was proud of them. I am proud to be an American.

I turned to Elvis and we locked eyes for a second and then began another run through the narrow street back to our helicopter. Cyrus had the bird running and ready for takeoff the instant we buckled in, and we flew directly to LZ Washington. There was no need to speak about the bodies. All the blood on my hands and clothes, with the look on my face, told the story.

At this point I felt the army had control of the situation with their Apache helicopters and Stryker vehicles, so I made a radio call to all Blackwater aircraft to RTB (Return To Base). Who would have known that things would quickly change again?

All four Blackwater helicopters arrived back at the LZ (Landing Zone), and we began a damage assessment. Before we completed it, we received another radio call that two of our Blackwater ground teams had come under attack again and were requesting air support. Once again, with no hesitation, two of the Little Bird crews dropped everything they were doing, loaded up and flew back into danger in support of the ground teams. Over the next twenty-four hours, hundreds of insurgents were killed or captured by U.S. forces.

I stayed on the ground because I felt some urgency to report the status to my boss. I walked to a secluded area where I could make a series of phone calls, first to the Chief Pilot for Blackwater. He lived in Moyock, North Carolina and had been a friend for many years. The conversation was short. I gave him the major details and told him I would write a full report. He then called the President of Blackwater Aviation.

I struggled to force myself to make the worst of the phone calls. I called my wife Deonna, first but only spent a couple of minutes explaining what had happened. I needed to talk with her to get the strength to make the next two phone calls to my mother and then to Art's wife.

The shock and grief they each expressed after learning that Art had been killed was unquenchable. I told them Art had just been killed in combat moments ago and that it happened quickly, without suffering. As I hung up the phone, I noticed how much blood was all over my hands, arms and front. I went to my room and cleaned up.

The news about the death of the door gunner on 3-3 and the four crewmen on 3-4 began to spread around. I began receiving phone calls from friends and coworkers from all over the globe. Some of my old buddies who were still serving in Special Operations units near Baghdad came to offer their condolences.

Every time someone said they were sorry to hear about my brother Art, I reminded them, "Thank you, but don't forget that we lost five brothers today."

They shook my hand warmly, hugged briefly, and said, "Roger that brother."

At my nightly 7:00 PM meeting, all the Blackwater Aviation personnel were there and I thanked them for the courageous manner in which they handled the events of that day. None of them had hesitated for a second to go into harm's way. I let them know that it was an honor and privilege to work with all of them. They assumed I would be leaving with my brother's body to escort him back home, but I made it clear that I still had a job to do and would not leave until a replacement was sent to take my place. I also made it clear that I would be coming back after the funeral.

After the meeting, I was asked to meet with U.S. Ambassador Zalmay Khalilzad at the morgue; a security team drove me there. Upon my arrival, I was escorted into the room where the bodies had been laid on tables.

The doctor asked, "Would you like to be alone with them?"

I said, "Yes sir, thank you."

The bodies had been cleaned up. I went to each of them: Arthur Laguna, Ron Johnson, Shane Stanfield, Steve Gernet and Casey Cassavant. I put my hand on each of their foreheads hoping they could feel my love and respect. As I stood at the side of my brother, I felt sorrow and guilt for his death.

A few minutes later there was a knock at the door and Ambassador

Khalilzad walked in and grabbed my hand, saying, "I am so sorry for the loss of your men. I knew your brother, as he had escorted and flown me a number of times."

Because I appreciated his sincerity, I held tightly to his hand. "Thank you, my brother is in a better place now."

Ambassador Zalmay Khalilzad, was the U. S. Ambassador to Iraq from June 2005 to April of 2007, when he began service as the U. S. Representative to the United Nations. He is a man I knew well, but I was still surprised and pleased to hear his response. "How great your joy will be when you meet him again."

I have always been impressed that he is a man of true compassion and moral fiber. He went to each of my friends and placed his hand on their foreheads and pronounced what seemed to be a prayer.

The morning after Art was killed, unable to sleep, I got up early and went to my brother's room to start packing his stuff. It was gut wrenching, and I could only stand to be in his room a few minutes at a time. Some of the guys asked if I wanted them to pack his stuff for me. I thanked them and told them that I would get it done. I know they could see the rough time I was having, but I wanted to be the one to do it. It actually took me three days to pack all his personal items. I called his wife, Mary, to see if there was anything in particular she wanted. She suggested I pass out all the Aloha shirts to all the guys in Blackwater Aviation.

When I took over the job as Aviation Manager in Baghdad near the end of 2005, I decided to have Aloha Fridays as a way to break up the week and maintain morale. Everyone was allowed to wear Hawaiian shirts on that day. Art had loved Aloha Friday. It had been his favorite day of the week, and he had nearly twenty Aloha shirts. Everyone knew how much he had loved those Fridays, so they had begun to tease him about it. Humor was a great way to help everyone endure the stress of our jobs.

On Art's first Aloha Friday in Baghdad, my Assistant Manager asked, "How many of you think Art's shirt is an authentic Hawaiian shirt? Show a thumbs-up."

Everyone immediately did a thumbs-down, joking that Art's shirt was not an authentic Hawaiian shirt. Art would call back home and tell our mom and Mary about being voted down and that he needed a real Hawaiian shirt. This went on week after week. Mom and Mary went to all the stores trying to find authentic Hawaiian shirts. That was why he had so many of them. Now I and the other guys wear them in his honor.

It wasn't until five days later that my replacement arrived and I was able to fly home. Our five brothers killed in action were flown on military aircraft back to the States, landing first in Dover, Delaware, where their bodies were prepared to be flown to their home state for a funeral.

To this day I still wonder if I did the right thing by not escorting Art's body to the U.S. from Baghdad. The decision I made still haunts me that he flew back to the U.S. alone, but I had men still in harm's way and felt I was needed there as well.

When I was finally able to fly to the U.S. to meet up with Art's body, I had hours and hours to think of that horrific day. I could not escape the "what-ifs" that began to run through my head over and over again. I will never forgive myself for Art's death. I just wished it had been me who died on that terrible day instead of my friends. Unless you have been faced with the responsibility of so many lives, you will never understand the emotions that you have to deal with. I am sure I will be haunted with the what-ifs the rest of my life.

It was a very long plane ride to the U.S. It seemed to me all the passengers knew my plight and were very courteous and warm towards me. I was offered food but had no appetite at all. When I arrived in the States, I met up with Deonna. The second I saw her, I felt embarrassed and ashamed that I was doing something that Art would never be able to do again: be with his family.

Deonna and I finally met up with my younger brother Milo and a fellow guardsman, Sgt. Clinton. They were to help escort Art's body home. Milo had been in the same Guard unit as Art so they had sent him to help. We ensured Art's body was loaded on the airplane for the long ride to Sacramento. The captain of the airplane had Deonna, Milo, Sgt. Clinton and myself load before all the other passengers. Before the airplane took off, the captain announced that this was a very important flight. He stated that there was a war hero on board who had died for his country in Iraq and was being escorted home by his brothers.

On the journey home, I was asked many times how Art was killed. I told them he was my wingman on a mission to help save a female diplomat in harm's way and that he was shot down protecting her. After they found out the circumstances of his death, some would say, "I am sorry for your loss." Some would start crying, and some would just turn and walk away speechless.

Just prior to landing in Chicago, the captain made an announcement and asked if everyone could remain seated after we had landed so the escorts could deplane and complete their duties. Also, just prior to landing, one of the flight attendants gave me a handful of napkins. Each of the passengers had written their heartfelt condolences on them, which I later gave to Art's wife.

At the Chicago airport, an airline employee had gone to great personal expense to construct a special trailer that was used exclusively to carry the caskets of those killed in combat. It felt good to see that kind of respect shown to our military men and women. I don't know if I have ever been more proud to be an American than I was at that moment. It didn't matter if they supported the war or not. They all seemed to be indebted to my brother for his service to his country and for their freedom.

The last stop was Sacramento, California. The only place that we did not receive a warm welcome was in our own hometown of Sacramento. The captain of the airplane was not allowed to let the escorts deplane and provide the proper respect to one of their own. The airport manager and authorities said that it was not their concern, that everyone on board would have to comply with their request and debark as usual and that Art's body would be offloaded with the rest of the cargo. Sacramento could not have shown any more disrespect for a fallen hero, who was one of their own, if they tried.

CHAPTER THREE
Reflections of Youth

AFTER REFLECTING ON THE EVENTS leading to Art's death my mind slowly returned to the present. I was struggling to keep my mind from wandering. I often felt dazed and confused. Funerals are usually over when everyone leaves the graveside, but most of the people in our long string of cars were going back to the church for a luncheon. It is a tradition, so to speak, of the LDS community. Friends and family gather to reminisce. A few impatient drivers showed their frustration when they were delayed because of the cars leaving the cemetery. I wished the impatient ones had understood the kind of man we had just buried.

The drive from the cemetery to the church luncheon was slow. There was a long line of cars patiently waiting their turn to pull out and follow the lead car. I hadn't spoken a word but Deonna knew what I was thinking.

She reached for my hand and reassured me, "I know this is hard and I wish you didn't have to go through it. I would do anything to make this go away, but I can't."

I nodded but didn't feel like saying anything. I felt responsible for my brother's death and no amount of talking could change that. We held hands as the line of cars moved away from the cemetery.

The sounds of cars motoring and honking along Marysville Boulevard began to distract my mind from the bad memories of the way Art died. Deonna and I moved along with the traffic and eventually happy visions of growing up with my brothers replaced the mournful memories of the scene of death from only a week earlier.

Art and Milo were more than just brothers to me. They were more than just family. My brothers were my best friends. Living on a five-acre farm in the country, we didn't have a lot of other friends. My parents wanted it that way. We grew up living life to its fullest degree, always looking out for one another. I do have another brother, Rick, who is many years younger than I, so he was too young to do the same things that my other two brothers and I were doing.

I also have three sisters who are younger than I am: Annette, Linda, and Mona. I remember braiding their hair and helping my mother get them ready for school. Our family was close, and I loved all my brothers and sisters, however, Art and Milo were closer in age and we had the same interests. We had done everything together.

As we drove along Deonna noticed a smile on my face. She asked, "What are you smiling about?"

"I was just remembering a time when my brothers and I played 'Combat' using BB guns."

Combat was an old television series about a platoon of men during World War II. It played in the early 1960s and was a favorite program of ours. My dad always watched it with us, and that was where we had gotten the idea of playing war with BB guns.

She feigned disgust but was actually pleased to hear me talking freely and showing better spirits.

I continued, "We dug foxholes and were shooting at each other from across the field one day when I shot Milo right between the eyes."

Her response reminded me of the old classic movie *A Christmas Story,* where the little boy wanted a BB gun for Christmas and his mother told him, "You'll shoot your eye out!"

Deonna exclaimed, "You guys are lucky you didn't shoot somebody's eye out! You guys are crazy! Did your mom know what you were doing?"

I chuckled. "She did that time. The BB stuck in his forehead and mom had to pry it out. He still has the scar."

We laughed, and it felt good to recall these fond childhood memories. Deonna smiled and shook her head, happy to see me recalling happier times.

She asked, "Remember the time you ran over Art with your motorcycle?"

"Oh yeah," I said, "that was the day we went riding in the Kahuku Mountains when we were stationed in Hawaii together. Art was wearing a white T-shirt that day and while racing up the mountain he crashed in front of me. I couldn't stop in time so I ran right over the top of him leaving a muddy tire track across his back."

Deonna chuckled. "When you guys came home he was walking kind of hunched over and I asked him what happened." He smiled sheepishly and said, "Danny ran over me." Deonna said, "You know, I don't think I've ever seen Art mad. He was always such an easygoing guy."

Deonna reached over to hold my hand, and as we smiled and continued our drive to the luncheon at the church, my mind continued to earlier times in my life.

There was a time when my brothers and I were in the Boy Scouts together. One weekend our scout troop went on a camping trip by a lake near Mt. Whitney in California. The lake was brutally cold and all of the older scouts were working on their swimming merit badge, which required a one-mile swim. They were swimming across the lake, but I was only eleven years old so the leaders wanted me to wait until I was older before I tried the long swim. I insisted that they let me swim and finally got what I wanted. I jumped into the water, and the shock of the cold water took my breath away.

The leaders kept encouraging me until they saw how cold and exhausted I was, and they began asking me to stop and get in the boat. I refused. Eventually, I swam the entire mile and was proud of myself for the accomplishment. The swim across that frigid lake was one of the most difficult things I had ever done to that point. When I arrived home, I ran straight to my dad and told him what I had done. His hearty approval meant a lot to me.

My mother taught me to always be prepared. When I would go camping with the Boy Scouts or with friends, my mother would make sure I was prepared with matches, a fishing line, a pocketknife, a whistle, a plastic bag for an improvised shelter and much more. To this day even if I go on a day hike, I take enough stuff with me to survive for at least seventy-two hours. The things I have learned from my mother about being prepared helped me as a Survival Instructor for Special Forces as well as a Scout Master. I have passed this knowledge on to my own children and grandchildren. As the old saying goes, "Mother knows best."

A flood of happy memories continued to flow into my mind about the great days of my youth. Our dad was a tough old guy who truly wanted to make a career out of the military. We were a very patriotic family and always displayed the American flag. Dad loved our country and that love of country and flag became an important part of our lives.

If he had not been wounded so badly by a landmine in Korea, Dad would have stayed in the army. It was what he really wanted. He always talked about joining the Special Forces and wearing the Green Beret. His disappointment was evident every time he spoke of what "might have been." Whenever a war movie was showing on television, Dad would gather us boys to enjoy it together.

Dad spent years recovering from his war wounds. We often drove to San Francisco to the Veteran's Hospital where my dad received treatment. He had to wear special boots because his injured right leg was a couple of inches shorter than the left leg. The doctors told him that he was fortunate he was to have avoided amputation.

Dad often joked about his encounter with the landmine saying, "I cussed all the way up and prayed all the way down."

With Dad's injuries he was in and out of the hospital quite a bit and would sometimes go unemployed. I remembered as a young boy riding with my aunt and uncle to various locations to pick tomatoes with the migrant workers. We worked very long days picking tomatoes and stacking the boxes, row after row. We seldom stopped for lunch but would eat tomatoes and sometimes had a sandwich in our pocket that we'd eat while we continued to work. What little money I earned I gave eagerly to my mom. It was hard work for a young boy, but it made me a better person.

Dad's disability made it difficult sometimes for him to find employment, but he often did auto-body work. That was how we ended up with a junk car that my brothers and I drove around our five acres. We had motorcycles as well, and one summer we built a ramp to jump over the old car. More than once we collided in midair on those motorcycles, falling to the ground laughing. Getting hurt was just a side effect of having loads of fun.

My mischievous boyhood memories began flooding my mind, as if it were yesterday. I remembered a time when my brothers and I were playing darts. I threw all the darts but one. I held one dart behind my back and waited for Milo to walk up to the dartboard and pull the other darts out. He kept telling me that one was missing, but I insisted they were all there. Just as he reached for the board, I threw my hidden dart. It punctured his hand and pinned him to the dartboard. He didn't think it was too funny back then, but we laugh about it today.

Another time the three of us were making a tree fort in some fig trees on our property. There were five fig trees in a row about ten to fifteen feet apart. We were always trying to improve on our tree fort by extending it to another tree. I was attempting to jump from one tree to the other by jumping and grabbing a rope so I could swing myself to the other tree. This foolish attempt comes from watching too many Tarzan movies. As I stood there on the tree limb about fifteen feet above the ground, I tried to build up the courage to jump. I gave it the one, two, three, go! I found myself hesitating more than once. Finally I gained enough courage to jump. With my brothers calling me a wimp I took a deep breath, yelled "Geronimo!" and jumped. As my feet left the branch of the tree, I realized I had a nanosecond of hesitation and knew that I would not reach the rope. With everything I had in me, I stretched out my hand, hoping to be able to grab the rope, but as I fell I could feel the rope at my fingertips with no chance of grabbing it.

As I fell crashing through some tree branches, one of those branches snagged my eye, pulling it out of its socket. I raced to the house with my brothers running alongside me in horror. My poor mom was shocked to see what we had done this time and quickly drove me to the hospital. Even as I recovered from that injury, wearing an eye patch, we continued our adventurous fun. I suppose we were reckless but what great memories I have of those early years in my life.

As I continued to daydream I recalled a day in 1968 when I was fifteen; a John Wayne movie was playing at the old 49er Drive-In Theater just across the street from the cemetery where Art and my father were later buried. My dad took my brothers and me to the drive-in where we watched the movie that changed my life. We all sat crunched in the front seat of my dad's Ford truck, ate popcorn, and watched *The Green Berets* on the big screen. We laughed, trembled, and sat wide-eyed as John Wayne played the soldier hero of my all-time-favorite movie.

My dad would make comments throughout the movie, saying,

"If I didn't get hurt in Korea this is what I would have done in the army."

I left the drive-in that night with a firm determination to join the army and become a Green Beret, thinking I needed to do this for my dad.

While we were growing up, my mother tried to instill religion in all of us. Religion was an important aspect of our lives. My family was Catholic and we attended church regularly. I even studied Latin to become an altar boy. We all believed in God and never questioned the fact that God lived and that our blessings were from Him. However, we occasionally listened to different religious messengers who would stop by our house.

We studied the Bible with the Jehovah's Witnesses. I remember running home from school to change clothes and get ready for them to come and teach us to read the Bible. It was something I looked forward to doing. During our studies I found out they did not believe in going in the army or defending our country. That was the turning point for me in my studies with them. I knew that I was going to go in the army someday, and if they didn't believe in defending our country, that religion was not for me. But I will always be grateful to them for teaching me the Bible and improving my ability to read.

My mother's good friend, Ann LaForte, was Mormon. She was very kind and soft-spoken and truly cared for my mother. One day my mother announced that we would be having a visit from some Mormon missionaries. I didn't really want to meet the missionaries and wasn't even sure what a missionary was, but they showed up one day. Elder Villa and Elder Polson didn't start out reading the Bible to us or even discussing religion. Instead they talked and joked around with us and became our friends. They were always willing to play a game of basketball, even in their suits, and we began to look forward to their visits.

As soon as I learned that Mormons didn't believe in drinking alcohol or smoking, I became all the more interested in learning about their church. We took the discussions and it wasn't long before we all agreed to become baptized into the Church of Jesus Christ of Latter Day Saints, the Mormons. I've been very happy with my decision to belong to this church, and I truly believe that my understanding and faith in a loving Heavenly Father has helped me endure the many days of distress and anguish I later experienced in my life.

I started attending the LDS (Mormon) church, which is where I met a beautiful blonde girl named Deonna Forsyth. We were only sixteen when I first saw her while I was playing basketball in the church gymnasium. She was there practicing for a play and it turned out they were short one person for a dance scene. Although we were both shy, she looked around for a dance partner and our eyes met.

She immediately walked over to me and said, "You can be my partner!"

Deonna is the first and only girlfriend I have ever had. We fell in love at sixteen and have been together ever since. I was star struck when I first saw her. She is what I thank God for most in my life. Without her I could not have been able to accomplish the things that I have. She supports me in the things I want to do with my life. They say that behind every good man is a good woman. I would not have our five wonderful children and all the wonderful memories of our children growing up if not for her. She is my best friend and the person I want to spend eternity with. My every waking moment is spent waiting to be with her again. No one makes me as happy as she does. I am more than blessed to have such a beautiful, loving, and caring wife to share my dreams and life with.

Memories of my mom's father, Merced Santoyo, who lived with us as I was growing up, began to play in my mind. I shared a bedroom with Grandpa and loved him tremendously. He was a Mexican Indian and knew a lot about nature and how to survive off the land. Grandpa showed my brothers and me how to trap and snare animals and which plants were edible.

My grandfather and grandmother on my dad's side, Arturo Llaguno and Concepcion Llaguno, were Yaqui Indians. He and my grandma immigrated to America before my father was born. My father's birth certificate shows his last name as Llaguno but when he and his siblings went to school their last name was changed to Laguna. The school administrators didn't like the double L in our name and therefore dropped one of them and changed the **o** at the end to an **a** to Americanize our last name. Since my grandparents didn't speak English, they couldn't protest it effectively and just let it happen. A few of my father's older siblings were born in Mexico and kept the original last name of Llaguno.

The Yaqui Indians were from northern Sonora Mexico, and southern Arizona. They were a fierce tribe and had lived off the land for years.

I remember the patience it took to snare quail. When I finally caught one, Grandpa Santoyo taught me to eat all the edible parts of the bird. He would dig in the bird's throat and eat the seeds stored there and then search the bird's insides for undeveloped eggs, which were also eaten. All the survival things my Grandpa Santoyo taught me later helped me in Special Forces School.

Grandpa Santoyo worked as hard as anyone I've ever known. Every spring he would plow two acres of our land with nothing but a shovel and then plant the entire field by hand. His gardening gave him great pride and as we labored in the garden with him, we learned an important lesson: we reap what we sow.

I was close to my grandfather and could tell he cared for me immensely. I recalled a time when Deonna and I were dating and my grandpa gathered a large paper bag full of walnuts from our tree and shelled them. He came to me and told me they were for my sweetheart. Grandpa liked Deonna but thought she was too skinny and was always trying to get her to eat. Grandpa didn't speak English so he couldn't communicate with Deonna but knew she was good to me and made me happy. When I joined the army and left home, Grandpa stood by the house and wept like a child.

As a minority growing up in the 1960's, I had to deal with people who were prejudiced. Both of my parents were Native American and most people stereotyped us as being second-class citizens. I attended Rio Linda Senior High School where there were not many minorities. I can recall on more than one occasion when a high school teacher told me that I would most likely end up spending time in prison or flipping burgers for a living. Nobody believed that my brothers and I would ever amount to anything. Those comments only served to make me more determined than ever to prove them wrong. For the most part I would ignore the prejudicial comments and racial slurs.

After I graduated from high school, I spent one semester at American River College. On April 19, 1972 while on my way home from classes, I did what I always knew I would do some day. Deonna and I drove past a U.S. Army recruiting station everyday as we went to and from the campus, and that day, I stopped and walked into the office. I told the recruiter that I was ready to volunteer for the army, and that I wanted to go into the infantry. They asked me how soon I wanted to leave and I told them as soon as they had an opening for me. The recruiter smiled and told me I could be on a bus that same day and I agreed to that. Deonna was not happy but she always knew I would be a soldier and reluctantly accepted what I had done. We made plans to get married as soon as I graduated from Basic Training and AIT (Advanced Infantry Training).

A few hours later I told my mother of my decision, and she lost her breath and had to sit down. A little later my father came home and I told him what I had done.

He said, "I sure hope you know what you're doing."

I packed my bags and the whole family rode with me to the bus station. I didn't have any feeling of reluctance. I knew this was what I was meant to do. My only apprehension was not being able to see Deonna for a few months. After a tearful separation I was on my way to a career that would take me on a bittersweet journey.

As we continued following the cars to the church to attend the luncheon that was prepared by members of our church for close family and friends, the day seemed especially warm for February, so I turned on the air conditioner.

That unusually warm day reminded me of those hot days and nights in Iraq. In the back of my mind I was thinking about my guys back in Iraq. It was a particularly violent period in Baghdad, with a lot of attacks and roadside bombings. Insurgents were causing horrific numbers of senseless deaths. I knew that the air and ground missions of Blackwater were getting more and more dangerous.

Although I was glad to be home I felt a responsibility to get back to Baghdad.

I also felt bad that I could not attend the funerals of the other four men I considered my brothers and who had been killed on the same mission as Art. Thoughts of them drifted in and out of my head throughout the day. But I had a bigger duty and that was to my own brother and family. I can't begin to describe the anguish of feeling like I was not there for the families of those four brave heroes who had died alongside my brother Art.

Deonna put her hand on mine. I had gotten lost in my thoughts and quit talking. Grateful to have her by my side I looked at her and said, "There are so many memories."

I was silent as I considered the three decades we had been married. I looked at Deonna. Her kindness was warm and thoughtful. After a moment, I said, "I like thinking of the old days. We've had a great life, haven't we?"

"The best, Danny. We've had the best." Deonna, still holding my hand, gave it a squeeze, and I drifted away into more memories.

CHAPTER FOUR
Army Life

As we drove along, I forced myself to think of other things, so I began thinking about the early days of my military career. One morning during the first two days of my Basic Training the Drill Sergeant had a uniform inspection. The inspection went fine up to the point when the Drill Sergeant asked me why I had not shaved.

I must have given him a puzzled look and then I said, "Drill Sergeant, I have never shaved and have nothing to shave."

He laughed and said, "Private, all soldiers shave in this man's army. Now get in the barracks and shave."

As I was running to go shave he yelled, "And you better shave every morning soldier!"

I ran straight to my duffle bag and dug to the bottom where I had a razor not thinking I would ever really have to use it. Without shaving cream and only using water, I went to work. By the time I was done shaving, it looked like I had gotten into a fight with a mountain lion.

I had spots of blood all over my face, and it did not help that the Drill Sergeant had not given me much time. This was just one of many experiences I endured during Basic Training.

The only negative experience I can remember while in Basic Training was the day I was qualifying on the M16 firing range. On one of the last days for qualification, my M16 jammed. I did the emergency action procedure as I was taught but the M16 was still jammed. So as instructed in our safety class prior to going to the range, I raised my hand and kept the M16 pointed down range. The Drill Sergeant came over to my position, yelling and screaming my name. "Private Laguna, what the **** is the problem?"

I immediately told him my weapon had jammed and that I did the emergency action procedure as taught. He very quickly grabbed the M16 out of my hand and kicked the charging handle forward (a part of the upper receiver that assists the bolt to go forward). He then handed my M16 back to me and told me to hurry up and shoot.

As soon as I pulled the trigger, my M16 blew up in my face. The next thing I remember, I was lying on my back with the Drill Sergeant yelling at me again. The only good thing about my weapon blowing up was that my ears were ringing and I could not hear what the Drill Sergeant was yelling. Other than some minor cuts to my face, I was unscathed.

During Basic Training I had a lot of experiences that helped prepare me for the next step of training which would focus more on my chosen MOS (Military Occupational Specialty) as an Infantry soldier. AIT (Advanced Infantry Training) seemed to be a little harder than Basic Training but a lot more fun. I adapted to army life very well.

A couple of days prior to graduating from AIT, the Drill Sergeant told me I had to go see the commander.

I immediately thought, *what did I do now?*

I reported to the commander as directed by the Drill Sergeant with a knock on his door.

He said, "Come in."

I walked in, stood in front of his desk and saluted.

He said, "Stand at ease."

I immediately snapped to parade rest. Lucky for me it was early in the morning and my fatigues hadn't gotten dirty or wrinkled yet.

His first question was "Do you always look like that?"

I replied to him, "Yes, sir."

He said "Good."

Then he asked me a bunch of questions like the maximum effective range of my M16, my general orders, and a bunch of other questions on things we learned in AIT.

One of his last questions was, "What do you think about the United States Army?"

I started off with saying, "My father and his brother served this country." I then said, "My two uncles whom I have never met, died doing so." I told him a little about my father and the injuries he had received from combat and how he had been highly decorated. I also told him that I wanted to make my parents proud of me, and if I could, I would sign up right now for twenty years. He just laughed.

He said, "Because of your performance here in AIT, you will be representing us as the Honor Graduate."

I was picked from more than one hundred and fifty other guys. I felt like I was floating when he said, "Dismissed."

I saluted him and left. The Drill Sergeant was waiting outside the door to congratulate me.

He said, "Take the rest of the day and get your uniform prepared with your new rank. You have just been promoted to Private First Class (PFC)."

In the enlisted ranks (E-1 through E-9) PFC is E-3. I don't think anyone will ever know how I felt that day.

I remembered going home after my Basic Training and Advanced Infantry Training. I couldn't get home fast enough; I wanted to give my dad the trophy I had received for graduating as the Honor Graduate. Dad was proud of me and hugged me hard. Hugs from him were rare and appreciated. Grandpa Santoyo threw his arms around me and was as excited as a little kid to see me.

Being Honor Graduate gave me a rank advancement as well as the opportunity to be a hometown recruiter for two months. The best part was that a hometown recruiter got paid an additional twenty-five dollars a day. That was a huge amount of money to me.

After Basic Training and Advanced Infantry Training, I came home and married my high school sweetheart, determined to prove to everyone that I would be a good husband, father and career soldier. I felt I had it all. There couldn't be anything better than to be married to the woman of my dreams and start a new career in the army.

My first duty station was at Schofield Army Barracks in Hawaii. It took several months to save enough money to buy an airplane ticket for Deonna to join me and to find an apartment to rent. Deonna worked at a department store and saved money to come and be with me. I only earned about $200 a month at that time. I didn't have enough rank yet to become command sponsored, so the army didn't pay for Deonna's move to Hawaii.

Deonna arrived in Hawaii on December 7, 1972, a day that will live in infamy. (Just a little joke there) I met her at the Honolulu airport. I went to the airport several hours early because I just couldn't wait. When I finally saw her walk off the airplane, my heart started pounding so hard I thought it was going to jump out of my chest. She was more beautiful than I had remembered. I ran up to her and put a Hawaiian lei around her neck, kissed her and gave her a big hug. I didn't want to let go. This was to be the start of our new life together.

I bought a junky old car and we shared an apartment with another newly wed couple. We could barely survive on what little income we had and to make matters worse, the army messed up my pay. Back in those days you were only paid once a month, so when I didn't get paid that month, it meant we went two months without getting paid. We used our savings to pay the rent and utilities but went without much to eat. We had one box of oatmeal, a box of brown sugar and a can of condensed milk and did everything we could to make it last as long as possible.

Every week my infantry unit went on field exercises for two or three days. I was given three boxes of C-rations each day, but I only ate one meal a day and saved the other two meals to take home. There were a lot of hungry hours during that time.

One day I pulled the car seats out of the car looking for loose change that may have fallen between the cushions from the previous owner. I found fifteen cents, so Deonna and I sat around for an hour trying to decide how best to spend it. We finally decided to buy a loaf of bread. We had nothing to put on the bread, so we ate it plain and enjoyed every bite.

We attended church in a little Mormon chapel in Wahiawa, Hawaii. The people there were wonderful to us. The time we spent with our new friends made up some of our best memories. We were too proud to let anyone know of our problem; but the Lord knew and

He blessed us. We had many invitations to dinner over the weeks by several different families within our ward. Mormons call their congregations wards.

When we were finally paid our two months of back pay we rejoiced. This experience helped us both to grow and become stronger. We learned many lessons about endurance and faith in God during these months. That experience in Hawaii for Deonna and me, poor as church mice the whole time, taught us to grow and mature as a couple and to depend on and support each other when times got rough. Deonna and I will never forget the many friends who helped us in our time of need and didn't even know they were doing anything special.

After several months of money problems and no food in the house Deonna became ill. We thought she had the flu but after several days she didn't recover, so I took her to the Emergency Room. The doctor gave her a pregnancy test and some medicine to help with the nausea. After several months of trying unsuccessfully to get pregnant, we began to think we couldn't have children. So when Deonna took the pregnancy test we didn't think it would come back positive.

Back then we couldn't afford a phone in our apartment so I had to call three days later from my work to get the results. The nurse confirmed that the test had come back positive, and I started stuttering and couldn't think what to ask her next. She continued with instructions on Deonna's first OB appointment and what to bring, but I was too excited and began jumping around like a kid at a circus. The nurse just laughed and told me to take a deep breath and count to ten.

Because we didn't have a phone, Deonna didn't find out about the good news until I came home later that day. We were so happy with the news of our first child and Deonna told me it wasn't fair that I knew before she did. I just laughed and let her know that there were quite a few guys standing in the office when I made that call and that they all knew. In fact, I was so excited I think the entire company knew before she did.

Our friends Richard and Leslie Clark invited us to stay with them while we waited for an apartment within our budget to become available. We put our name on a list for subsidized housing and an apartment became available a few months before our baby was born. It was a small place however, we lived alone, and it was wonderful to us. I had never been so happy.

We didn't have much, but we had no debt either. We never considered having a credit card and saved for months just to buy a small stereo. We bought very few clothes and if it wasn't for some church friends arranging for a baby shower, we probably wouldn't have had much for our baby. We managed to come across a crib that some friends in church were selling for eight dollars. I sanded it down and repainted it. On December 1st, 1973, Daniel Christopher Laguna was born. We called him Chris so there would be no confusion between father and son. Deonna's mom and sister, Carol came to help with the new family addition. Even though Deonna was the oldest of seven children, she felt overwhelmed and didn't know how to take care of a newborn baby. She was very happy her mother could come and help out.

Fifteen months later, we had a beautiful baby girl, Michelle Lena Laguna. Both Chris and Michelle were born in Tripler Army Medical Center in Hawaii. Our third child, another beautiful little girl, was conceived in Hawaii but born in Ft. Jackson, South Carolina. When our first child, was only two and a half years old we had our third baby. We named her Jamie Renae Laguna.

My brothers Art and Milo were stationed in Hawaii about a year after I had gotten there. As new soldiers in Hawaii, my brothers and I started skydiving. Deonna and the kids would come and watch me make three jumps every Saturday. One day I borrowed Milo's new parachute for a jump that nearly killed me. We jumped from army helicopters and that took a little more technique than a standard army parachute jump. As soon as I jumped, I started tumbling in the air. Still new at skydiving, I panicked and pulled the ripcord. The chute ejected as I was tumbling and wrapped around my right leg and right arm.

At first, falling through the sky, I panicked. It was a helpless feeling being wrapped up falling to a certain death; but an unexplainable calm came over me and I was able to think clearly. I knew what I needed to do to save my life. With my free hand, I grabbed the parachute and freed my arm and leg. The parachute started to look as though it was going to open but it tangled around itself. My only option at that point was to cut the parachute away. On each shoulder there is a canopy release system so you can cut away your parachute in an emergency.

As I accelerated to the earth, I cut the main chute away. The reserve parachute ripcord handle was attached to the main parachute so in the unlikely event you didn't get to your reserve handle quick enough it would open automatically for you. The reserve parachute was mounted on my chest, so when it inflated I was falling face up and in a very awkward landing position. Only seconds after my reserve parachute partially opened, I hit hard, slamming my head into the ground.

I remember lying on the ground looking up at the helicopter. The pilot flew down and hovered overhead to check on me. I held my hand in the air to let them know I was okay and they flew off. On this particular day, Deonna did not come to watch, and I was glad she wasn't there.

Milo drove up in his car and came running over to me. I was dazed and sick to my stomach, with a severe headache. He was yelling at me because he couldn't find his parachute and needed my help to search for it. He helped me up. I got in the car with him, and we drove around looking for his parachute. We couldn't find his parachute, and I was feeling very sick to my stomach. My head hurt badly. I finally convinced him to take me home. He reluctantly dropped me off at my apartment and went back to look for his parachute.

When I walked through the door holding my head, Deonna looked at me and said, "What's wrong? Did everything go okay?"

I said, "I had a parachute malfunction and I hit my head on the ground pretty hard. I have a headache and need to go lie down for a while."

She said, "Oh, no you're not! You are going to the hospital!"

I said, "I'll be all right. I just need to lie down."

She left the room and immediately called the emergency room and explained to them what had happened. They told her not to let me go to sleep and get me to the hospital as soon as possible. Deonna helped me to the car and drove me to the emergency room. They did a medical evaluation on me and then gave me something for my bad headache. One of the doctors asked me if I remembered what happened. I told him the whole story.

The doctor said, "You're a lucky man. I guess you won't skydive anymore will you?"

I said, "No sir, not until my head stops hurting."

He just shook his head and walked off.

I had a concussion and was supposed to go to Tripler Army Medical Center, which was at least a forty-minute drive. Tripler Army Medical Center was an enormous pink building that sat high on the mountain overlooking Honolulu. Tripler had been there since World War II. It was the hospital where my father was sent after he was wounded in Korea.

My parents were scheduled to visit us two days later, and I didn't want to be in the hospital when they arrived, so I lied to the doctors and told them Deonna would take me to Tripler. Then I lied to Deonna and told her I had a concussion but I was okay and the doctor said I could go home. So she took me home. I had bad headaches for a long time, and it was years later before Deonna heard the truth about that day. Needless to say she didn't like being lied to.

About a month after our second baby was born, my unit was deployed to Guam for "Operation New Life," the evacuation of Vietnamese refugees to Guam. I was reassigned from my unit to a Special Forces unit to work in this endeavor. My new title was Governor. As a Governor, I was in charge of more than seven thousand Vietnamese refugees. My job was to set up and provide in and out-processing for the refugees. I also setup baby care tents, first aid tents, clothes issuing points and mess halls. I was one of the only Americans allowed on the compound twenty-four hours a day while all the other soldiers worked eight-hour shifts and had to leave after their shifts ended.

You Have To Live Hard To Be Hard

I told my Special Forces boss I had a hard time communicating with the Vietnamese people and could not find anyone who could speak English. My boss told me to find someone to teach me the Vietnamese language. So I set out to find someone. I finally found a former Vietnamese military officer who could speak English very well. I told him I needed to learn to speak Vietnamese fast. He told me no problem *Trung si* (Vietnamese for sergeant).

The next day he brought two young Vietnamese women to my headquarters tent. He introduced them to me and said they would be happy to teach me. One of them was named Miss May. She started speaking to me in Spanish when she saw that my last name was Laguna. I answered her in English and told her I needed to learn Vietnamese.

She agreed to teach me the language and informed me that she could speak seven languages fluently. I spent the next couple of months doing my job and learning to read and speak Vietnamese. My interpreter would walk with me wherever I went to keep drilling me on the Vietnamese language. Within a month or so Miss May told me I was doing pretty well. I would always try to be the one to speak to the people first and when I messed up, she would help me.

One day I walked into a tent and overheard a group of Vietnamese men speaking. It appeared to me they were speaking in a different dialect. I motioned to my interpreters to follow me outside.

I asked my interpreters, "Why do they sound different to me?"

Miss May whispered to me that they were most likely North Vietnamese. I called security and they were detained. Later it was determined they were North Vietnamese soldiers who through all the confusion of the evacuation of the South Vietnamese were able to sneak themselves in with the rest of the refugees.

I enjoyed my duty there and enjoyed working with the Vietnamese people. Years later I still received a Christmas card from one of the former Vietnamese officers whom I had befriended.

During my time in Guam, working with the Special Forces soldiers made me all the more determined to become a Green Beret. I began working on getting accepted to Special Forces training. In those days a soldier had to have two years in the army before he could be considered as a candidate. The army had a high intelligence standard for acceptance into Green Beret training. Unfortunately, my test scores were too low to be admitted.

I was determined to meet the requirements, so I enrolled in a community college and began taking courses that would help improve my test scores. I went to school nearly every night for two years, very determined to let nothing stop me from attaining my goal.

After my three years in the 25th Infantry Division in Hawaii, my scores were finally high enough to qualify for admittance to Special Forces training, and I anxiously awaited my orders. Unfortunately, when my orders finally came, I discovered I would be spending the next two and a half years as a Drill Sergeant at the Army Basic Training School in Ft. Jackson, South Carolina. This was a huge disappointment, but I was determined to do my time in Ft. Jackson and then get my chance at earning the Green Beret.

Drill Sergeant Duty is very difficult on family life. Our third child, Jamie, was born six months after we arrived at Ft. Jackson, but I didn't see her much until she was nearly two years old. I didn't get home until after 9:30 every night and left every morning before 4:00 AM I even worked holidays and weekends.

I did my best as a Drill Sergeant, pushing the recruits very hard. We marched or ran everywhere we went, with me running right along with them. I didn't allow candy or cigarettes, and when my platoons graduated, they always scored highest in physical fitness.

One day while the recruits were standing at attention listening to my instructions a bird fell to the ground in front of me. Without thinking about it, I bent over and picked the bird up, and like my grandfather taught me, I bit its head off. That was how we killed the quail we would snare when I was a kid. Suddenly, a few recruits, already weak from running in the hot sun, began fainting.

Being a Drill Sergeant was more like being a babysitter. I remember a time when I ran to break up a fight between two soldiers. After I had separated them, one of them punched me hard on the side of the head, hitting me in my ear. My mind just went blank, and unfortunately for him, I had the right to defend myself. I had the option of pressing charges against him because he had hit me first; however, I figured he had paid the price already, so I elected to not press charges, and gave him another chance in the army. After that day, the other recruits were particularly well behaved.

Recruits were pushed hard by all the Drill Sergeants, because that was our job: to weed out the recruits who could not perform well in the army. One day we were running in formation, shouting cadence, when I noticed a young soldier dropping out and falling behind. I ran back to him and hollered for him to keep running. My intent was to help every recruit do his best. But this young man suddenly fell to the ground and died.

It turned out that the soldier had asthma but lied about it on his entry medical exam. I would not have pushed him so hard if I had known. Guys with asthma were not supposed to be in boot camp. I went home so upset about it that I couldn't even talk. It took hours before I could bring myself to explain to Deonna what had happened. The young soldier's death weighed heavily on me for a long time.

Although I was hard on my trainees, I know I did the best that I could and I wanted them to be the best they could be. Over the years, I have run into several of my former trainees who have done very well. In fact, I ran into one of them on a military Special Operations mission, and he was the Command Sergeant Major of the Second Ranger Battalion out of Fort Lewis, Washington.

It was obvious that a lot of time has passed since then, but when he yelled "Hey, sir," everyone in the briefing, turned around to look at him. We all thought he was addressing the Ranger Battalion Commander, but he was addressing me.

I asked, "Can I help you Sergeant Major?"

He asked, "Were you enlisted before?"

I said, "Yes Sergeant Major."

Then he asked, "Were you ever a Drill Sergeant?"

I replied, "Yes, Sergeant Major, but that was a very long time ago."

He said, "I know, you were my Drill Sergeant."

Everyone in the briefing room turned to me and said, "Dan, how old are you?"

My answer was, "I was just a good Drill Sergeant, and he was promoted very fast."

They all just laughed. The next day the Sergeant Major brought in his Basic Training Class Book to show me he wasn't joking. I remember sitting back and thinking, *twenty plus years-where did the time go?*

CHAPTER FIVE
Special Forces

IN THE SPRING OF 1978 I was finally selected for Special Forces training. My first stop was Airborne School in Ft. Benning, Georgia. I was already an experienced skydiver, having done many jumps with my brothers in Hawaii. Drill Sergeant Duty had put me in very good physical condition, so the Airborne School should have been very simple. But I made one mistake.

I arrived at Ft. Benning a couple of days before the class started, so I had time to go to the local skydiving club to see if I could make a couple of jumps before I started Army Airborne School. I walked in and found some guys standing around talking and others packing parachutes. I asked them if they would point me in the right direction so I could be put on the manifest to jump. After they checked my credentials, they offered me a parachute.

I told them, "No thanks, I've got my own."

One of them replied, "Roger that, see ya at the drop zone."

So off I went with my newly found friends and I made a couple of jumps.

Monday morning I was standing tall in formation at the Airborne School waiting for my name to be called to be placed in one of the platoons to start Airborne School.

When my name was finally called I gave a loud response "Here, Sergeant Airborne."

Well, as luck would have it, the cadre for our platoon was made up of the same guys I was skydiving with that prior Saturday. When I was running to fall into my position in the platoon, our eyes met and he had an evil smile on his face.

The entire cadre started yelling at me saying, "You want to be Airborne, Mr. Skydiver, beat your boots, Mr. Skydiver." *Beat your boots* was a punishment exercise given for the smallest infraction during training. From the standing position, you are required to squat, bending at the knees with your back remaining in the vertical position and your arms and hands hanging straight down. Each time you squat, you are required to slap the top of you boots, giving it the name "beat your boots." Typically, you would be required to do twenty to fifty of these.

I received that treatment until the day I graduated. After graduation the cadre told me it was all in fun and that was the first time they had jumped with someone who had more jumps than they had and was going through Airborne School. I thanked them for the special attention.

Every day I had to run several miles as part of the training. Normally, this would not have been a problem, because I was in very good shape and ran several miles a day. As luck would have it, somehow I injured my knee that prior Saturday making a skydiving jump, and it swelled up about twice its normal size. It was a requirement to complete Airborne School before going to Special Forces School. It was a concern because if I couldn't make the runs, I would be recycled and I would miss my class date for Special Forces School. It had always been my dream to go to Special Forces School and become a Green Beret, so if I had any choice in the matter, that wasn't going to happen. I managed to tough it out and made the runs anyway. I would go home at night and put ice on my knee to get the swelling to go down. I wrapped my knee with ace bandages and tried to hide the fact that I was injured. It hurt more to run than you'll ever know, but I forced myself to do it anyway. I couldn't go to the doctor because I didn't want to be recycled. I never set any record times on the runs, but I graduated Airborne School.

After I graduated from Airborne School, we learned that Deonna was expecting our fourth child. I also had a couple of weeks' break before I began Special Forces School, and during that time my knee started feeling better.

Special Forces School was approximately five months long. The school was broken into three phases, beginning with the most physically demanding part of the training. We learned hand-to-hand combat, land navigation, survival training, airborne operations, academic classes involving clandestine operations, and much more.

While I was going through Phase One of Special Forces School, I had a good friend named Gary. Gary was a great guy who became a very good Green Beret, but he had a weakness in physical endurance. Teamwork was encouraged during our training, and I would do whatever I needed to do to help my team members pass the course.

One day, we were on a long run with fifty-pound rucksacks on our backs. Gary was having a hard time, so I told him, "Grab on to the back of my rucksack. I'll pull you. Just keep your feet moving and hang on." We made it to the end of the run in good time.

During Phase Two of training, we were divided into groups according to our assigned specialty. As a Light and Heavy Weapons Expert, I was required to learn all the weapons of the world and become proficient in disassembling, assembling, and accurately firing them. We were then trained to go behind enemy lines to recruit, train, and equip indigenous forces for guerilla raids, conduct offensive raids, or invasions of enemy territories and maintain proficiency with all foreign light and heavy weapons.

In Phase Three: the final phase of Special Forces Training, we all came back together and simulated operating as a Special Forces "A Team." We formed twelve-man teams and were given a mission to plan. We went into isolation for about three days to plan the mission and then briefed our mission to the cadre. After we got a thumbs-up, we boarded a C-130 at night to be dropped into a remote location in the mountains of North Carolina. We jumped on Halloween night into a drop zone called DZ (Drop Zone) Death.

At the designated time during our Nap of the Earth Flight in a C-130, the Jump Master began bellowing the familiar Jump Master calls. The doors opened up, and the twelve of us shuffled to the door, and prepared to jump into the night sky. There was little or no visibility on the ground for night jumps, and the risk of injury was significant. But for our kind of warfare, it was essential to train in night airborne maneuvers. The roar of the engines and the rushing winds made it difficult to communicate, even when we were yelling only a few inches away from each other.

Each of us exited the C-130 into the cold night air. It took my team approximately fifteen minutes to rendezvous at our linkup point, which was in a cemetery. We then spent two weeks in the mountains operating as a Special Forces A Team, successfully completing our mock mission.

More than two hundred good men started in our Special Forces class, but fewer than sixty graduated. It was difficult and demanding work, but my determination to excel helped me to graduate at the top of my class. In November 1978, I stood in formation and was awarded the coveted Green Beret.

Special Forces Survival Training came easy to me because of all the things my Grandpa Santoyo had taught me. After I served on a Special Forces A Team, I became the Senior Survival Instructor at the Special Forces Survival School at Ft. Bragg, North Carolina. I worked under the command of Col. Nick Rowe, a former Vietnamese prisoner of war, and Col. Robert (Bob) Howard, a Congressional Medal of Honor recipient.

That proud moment was as much for my dad as it was for myself. The beret that was handed to me at graduation was the culmination of years of dreams and effort. After I graduated, I drove home to Rio Linda with my family for a short vacation, and gave the beret to my dad. It had been ten years since he took us to the 49er Drive-In to see John Wayne in the *The Green Berets*.

President Kennedy gave a speech at Ft. Bragg, North Carolina, on April 11, 1962. He was a huge supporter of Special Operations units and was responsible for allowing the Army Special Forces to wear a green beret rather than the standard army headgear.

In Kennedy's speech he said, "The Green Beret is a symbol of excellence, a badge of courage, a mark of distinction in the fight for freedom."

These men are among the finest fighting force in the world. They place their lives in danger much more often than the general public knows about and have paid a bloody price through the years. They are men of integrity, honor, loyalty, and courage, men who have undergone extreme mental, intellectual, and physical testing before they have proved themselves worthy of the fraternity. There is a unique sense of pride among those who have earned the right to wear the Green Beret.

Their missions are confidential and in many cases sensitive in nature. Brave soldiers are placing their lives in danger every day, somewhere around the world, but because the missions are unknown to the general public, their valorous efforts and stories of heroism are often untold.

My first assignment was in Panama with the 7th Special Forces Group. Fortunately, this was a tour that was authorized for families. On December 19, 1978, Deonna and I, with our three small children, boarded a plane to Howard Air Force Base in Panama.

After a long two and a half years as a Drill Sergeant, Panama was a welcome change. There was only one English-speaking television channel, and it played old re-runs like *I love Lucy*. My unit kept me busy with training, but we spent all of our free time doing family activities together. One of our favorite things was to take the kids to a remote location in the jungle to search for butterflies. We would try to catch huge blue butterflies, the most beautiful ones I had ever seen.

When I arrived at my first Special Forces A Team in Panama, everyone thought I spoke Spanish because of my last name. Greg Reyes, one of the guys on my team, would speak to me in Spanish, but I would answer him in English. He asked me if I knew how to speak Spanish, and I explained that my family spoke it and I that I understood it better than I spoke it. He started teasing me and told me that if I didn't start speaking Spanish he was going to start calling me Smith.

Not long after I arrived in Panama, I heard about a special unit that was being assembled. It would be responsible for more than the typical A Team missions. I volunteered for that new unit, known as Charlie 3-7. It is a Special Ops unit that performs missions in Central and South America. Everything about the unit at that time, except its name, was sensitive and close hold (which means it is not even disclosed to other A Teams). I spent two years there. It was known as the long hair unit, and I felt that I was born for the kind of operations we did. I was able to get a lot of training that most Special Operations teams did not have access to.

One of those schools was the Combat Divers School, perhaps the most demanding and difficult training I ever received. Approximately thirty Special Operations guys started the class, but only thirteen graduated. The class was extremely demanding, with very little sleep, and plenty of running and swimming. Our last day of class involved a seventeen-mile run at a very fast pace, followed by a long distance swim of 6.2 miles. There was a buoy about three miles out into the Atlantic Ocean. We had to swim to the buoy and back.

The families of the graduating class members were invited to the beach for a picnic but were told the first swimmers would not arrive for six hours. At the five-hour mark, some of the wives noticed the first swimmer already returning in record time. Deonna and some of the other wives ran down to the beach to see who was returning first, and she recognized me as I stood up in chest-deep water and approached the beach.

As I waded onto the beach exhausted, I began to lie down when the class instructor walked up to me and said, "Good job, but you're not done."

I looked at him, afraid to hear what was next.

The instructor continued, "Your final task is to do five hundred flutter kicks."

I rolled over, completed the flutter kicks and fell back onto the sand with no more strength. I had just graduated from Combat Divers School.

Later, as I enjoyed the picnic with the other guys and our families, one of the instructors approached me and asked, "How did you do it so fast?"

I smiled and replied, "There are a lot of sharks out there."

He smiled back and said, "*You Have To Live Hard To Be Hard.*"

That motto struck a chord in me. My dad hadn't raised me to be soft and neither had my grandfather or my mother. *You have to live hard to be hard.* I adopted it as my own personal motto.

Our fourth child, Jason Michael Laguna was born March 14, 1979. Deonna was a great mother and companion. She was happy to take the responsibility of a growing family, even with my frequent absences.

We lived in military housing and one of our neighbors was a lieutenant. I was an enlisted man in the Special Forces, and he was an officer in the regular infantry, so he had a grudge against me from the beginning. Officers sometimes feel they should not have to live in the same housing as enlisted personnel.

One day the Lieutenant took our daughter's tricycle and threw it onto the roof of the carport, because he was mad she had left it in his parking spot.

I went to see my boss, Captain Gary Harrell, a topnotch Special Operations Operator, now a retired Major General and former Delta

Force Commander. As I walked up to him in the Officer's Club, he said, "What's up, Dan? Is there something wrong?"

"Roger that, sir. I hate to bother you tonight; but I'm having a problem with my neighbor, and he's a Lieutenant."

After I explained the situation to him, he turned to his friend and said with a chuckle, "This won't take long. I'll be right back."

Captain Harrell stood up and waved for me to follow him. "Come on Dan. Let's go. I'll take care of this *Leg*." "Leg" is a disparaging term used to describe a non-airborne person.

Captain Harrell is a big, tough man, not the kind of guy you want to have a face-to-face confrontation with. When he got to my housing complex, he banged on the lieutenant's door and ordered him to come out.

The lieutenant came to the door and said, "Can I help you, sir?"

Captain Harrell shouted out his question. "Did you throw Sergeant Laguna's daughter's tricycle on the roof?"

The trembling young officer shyly answered, "Yes, sir."

"You have five minutes to get the bike back down!"

The lieutenant scrambled onto the roof and retrieved the bike, and then Captain Harrell said, "If you ever do something like that again, I will come back and rip your head off!"

"Yes, sir . . . got it" To this day, whenever I see Gary Harrell, I think of that poor lieutenant.

One day we were driving from the Atlantic side to the Pacific side of the Canal Zone to do some shopping. The other side had a bigger PX (Post Exchange) and better places to shop, so we planned a family day of fun and shopping. I had never driven the road before but had made the trip once with someone else driving, so I wasn't very familiar with the narrow winding road.

The road was literally in the middle of the jungle. I told the kids to watch out the car windows because you never knew what you might see. The jungles of Central America have monkeys, anteaters, boa constrictors, sloths, poisonous frogs, big luminescent butterflies and much more. When we would drive at night, the roads would be blanketed with frogs. They didn't sound like the frogs here in the United States. Instead of the recognizable 'ribbit' that we associated with frogs, we heard "boing, boing, boing."

Deonna laughed and said, "Even the frogs speak a different language here!" It was better than going to a zoo, and most of it was right in our backyard.

As I drove, I was watching for a certain turnoff that I remembered as a gradual turn, so I didn't think I needed to slow down in order to make the turn. When I unexpectedly came to the turn in the road, it was sharper than I remembered and had a high, steep cliff. I realized too late that we were traveling too fast to make the turn. Things seemed to move in slow motion and my life flashed before my eyes. The car spun around several times as we slid toward the cliff.

I remember thinking; *at least we will all die together.*

As the car spun around and then slowly rolled over toward the edge of the cliff, which was heavily wooded with jungle vegetation, the front of the car hit a tree about three inches in diameter. Nearby were Panamanians who suddenly came to our aid. They surrounded the car and balanced it so it would not shift left or right and tumble down the cliff. They pulled Deonna, who was seven months pregnant, and the kids out of the car. After they got my family safely out of the car, I walked around the entrance of the wooded area that led to a steep cliff and noticed it was mostly jungle brush. We hit the only tree large enough along that curve, that would stop us from going over the edge, and we managed to hit it direct on center.

The car was in a precarious balance and could have easily continued down the cliff with the slightest wrong movement. It was another miracle. The Panamanians spoke no English, but offered us water and were very kind and concerned about our welfare.

About five minutes later, an American drove by in a jeep and stopped to help us. He had a towing strap and pulled the car back onto the road. Our car only had a small dent on the nose of the hood and was otherwise undamaged.

When I got everyone back into the car, there was no one for me to thank. Just as fast as the Panamanians were there to help my family, they quickly all disappeared back into the jungle.

As we drove off, I said a silent prayer thanking Heavenly Father for our safety. We did finish our shopping trip and returned home safely.

We decided after our tour in Panama was over to get out of the army and try civilian life. We went back to our hometown in Rio Linda, California. My family opened a business doing auto-body and fender repair. My dad did that for a living, so Dad, Art, Milo, and I decided to open a shop of our own.

Deonna and I had our fifth and last child while there for that year. We named our little boy after both my grandfathers, Arturo Llaguno and Merced Santoyo. We named him Arthur Merced Laguna.

Our family business wasn't doing too well, so Deonna and I decided it was best that I go back into the army. About two months after our fifth child was born, I went to Ft. Bragg, North Carolina, back to Special Forces.

It took Deonna two long months to sell our car and rent the house out we had purchased while in Sacramento. Deonna and the kids were finally on their way to Fort Bragg. I was so happy to have my little family back with me. I went back in as a Sergeant (E-5), which was initially hard for me to accept because I had been on the Sergeant First Class (E-7) list when I decided to get out of the army. I made Staff Sergeant (E-6) within about six months and was on the Sergeant First Class (E-7) list again within that year. Some guys I worked with could not believe you could get promoted through the ranks that fast, but I did. This was just another blessing that I received from the Lord.

CHAPTER SIX
Flight School

After my time in Panama with Charlie Company 1st Battalion 7th Special Forces Group, referred to as Charlie 3-7, I was assigned as an Instructor at the Special Forces Warfare School in Fort Bragg, North Carolina. I had been promoted to Sergeant First Class and with the possibility in the not-too-distant future of another promotion. Within the Special Forces School, members of the cadre who were Master Sergeants or above would usually have a desk job. The last thing I wanted was to become a staff NCO. Some guys looked forward to the easier pace of an office worker, but I hated the idea.

Just prior to being assigned to Camp McCall at Ft. Bragg as a Special Forces Survival Instructor, my brother Art told me he had just applied for the army helicopter flight school program. He tried to get me to go to flight school, but I told him I wasn't interested.

In some brotherly bantering, he teased me saying, "You probably can't pass the flight aptitude test to be accepted anyway."

I laughed and said, "Art, if you can pass it, I can pass it."

Art continued the bantering, "I'll bet you a steak dinner you can't."

Because of our competitiveness and not ever wanting to lose a bet, I applied for the U. S. Army Flight School Training Program, essentially on a dare from Art. At first I didn't have any intention of actually going to flight school. I only applied to prove to Art that I could pass the flight aptitude test just as he did and that I could be qualified for acceptance.

Many months later, my brother Art brought my dad out to Fort Bragg for a visit on his way to Flight School. During their visit, I asked my dad if he would like to see where I worked. I took my dad out to Camp McCall where the Special Forces Warfare training center was located and introduced him to my boss, Colonel Nick Rowe, a long-time Green Beret who had spent over five years as a prisoner of war in Vietnam.

Colonel Rowe had graduated from West Point and had earned the right to wear a Green Beret and volunteered for service in Vietnam. He was captured in 1963 and held in a bamboo cage until 1968 when he finally saw an opportunity to escape. He overpowered his guards and began an escape and evasion that resulted in his rescue by a helicopter crew that had spotted him in the jungle. The helicopter crew flew down to kill him before they recognized that he was an American. Colonel Rowe was one of the very few American prisoners of war to have escaped Vietnamese imprisonment.

Colonel Rowe spent a lot of personal time with my dad and they swapped war stories. My dad received some special treatment and left there feeling better about his Korean War service, uplifted like I hadn't seen him in a long time. I always appreciated what Colonel Rowe did for my father that day making him feel like a war hero.

A few years after he visited with my dad, Colonel Rowe was assigned to the Philippines, where he was given the mission of Chief of the Army Division of the Joint U.S. Military Advisory Group (JUSMAG) providing counter-insurgency training for the Philippine military. On Friday, April 21, 1989, a band of terrorists pulled up along side his car and fired automatic weapons at point-blank range, killing the good man who had done so much for his country. He was buried in Arlington National Cemetery.

On the last day of their visit, my brother asked me if I had heard anything on my Flight School application.

I told him, "No, actually I forgot all about it." His question made me think, *I wonder what happened with the Flight School application I submitted almost a year ago.*

The next day while I was working at Camp McCall, I had some free time so I called the Department of the Army to see whatever became of my Flight School packet. When I finally got someone on the telephone at the Aviation Branch he asked me my social security number and full name.

After I gave it to him he said, "Hang on. I'll check it and get right back with you."

A few minutes later he picked up the telephone and said, "Yes I have your stuff right here in front of me, and from what I can see you should be reporting to Flight School at Fort Rucker in two weeks."

I almost fell out of my chair. After a pause, I said, "Are you sure? Because you could have me mixed up with my brother."

He asked, "Is your brother Arthur Laguna?"

I replied, "Yes sir, that's him."

He confirmed, "Well, you both will be in Flight School at the same time."

I still could not believe what I just heard. I asked him, "When was the Department of the Army going to let me know?"

He then told me, "Our records show we sent you Flight School orders over two months ago."

I said, "I have never received any orders."

He suggested, "Go down to Division Headquarters and by the time you get there I'll have a copy on the fax machine."

I quickly found Colonel Rowe and told him what was going on.

He said, "Now, that's just like the army."

I jumped in my car and quickly drove to Division Headquarters. Sure enough, the orders were there. I had really been accepted to Flight School, and had only a week to out process from Ft. Bragg. Deonna and I packed everything up, loaded our car, and moved to Ft. Rucker, Alabama. It was the quickest move we had ever made.

When we arrived at Fort Rucker, Alabama, I checked in with the Flight School cadre.

They saw that I was a Senior Non-Commissioned Officer and asked, "Are you sure this is what you really want?"

Most pilot trainees were younger guys, so it was unusual for a guy with my background to attempt flight training.

I said, "Yes sir, it is."

The cadre told me to go get my family settled and be back on start day ready to start Warrant Officer Career Development (WOC-D). When I left the building, I saw a group of flight school candidates walking in the Warrant Officer Candidate Training area. I stopped one of them and asked him if he knew my brother, Art Laguna.

He replied, "Yeah, he's in my class."

I asked, "Could you find him and have him meet me?"

A few minutes later Art came running up to me with his shaved head and no mustache, looking like a basic trainee.

With a big surprise on his face, he asked, "What are you doing here?" Before I could answer him, he said, "Did you come all this way to visit me?"

I said, "No, I'm here to start flight school with you." I told him what had happened after he had left and how I had found out about my orders to attend flight school.

Art laughed and said, "You didn't even want to fly helicopters!"

With a sense of pride I responded, "Hey, you challenged me. I told you I could make it to flight school."

Trainees didn't have the freedom to stand around talking, so Art had to leave. He said, "I have to go. I'm not supposed to have any visitors until the weekend."

As he walked away I hollered, "You owe me a steak dinner!"

Flight School was time-consuming and hard on the family. I spent the first couple months of flight school living in the barracks. We were not allowed to go home and be with our families. They visited once a week for a couple hours and that was it. This six-week program was designed to weed out the ones who had not committed themselves to the program. We lost quite a few classmates during those six weeks.

Toward the end of WOC-D, Art was getting ready for his final inspection before graduation. As a former Drill Sergeant, I had plenty of experience with inspections and knew exactly how to prepare my wall locker for a perfect inspection. Art didn't have that experience, so I decided to help him with his inspection. I switched out all of my clothes and spit-shined boots from my wall locker into his wall locker. Everything in the lockers had to be perfect, with clothes on hangars measured to the exact same measurement between each hanger. A sixteenth of an inch variation would be cause for demerits. The lid inside the can of boot polish had to be perfectly shined to a mirror finish. Our T-shirts had to be rolled a certain way with the last name showing. Because we had the same last name, I was able to bring my clothes and uniforms, with perfectly shined brass, to Art's wall locker. I set his locker up with careful attention to all the details, and Art passed his inspection with flying colors.

The only problem with my plan was that I now had Art's things in my wall locker, and had to go through the same inspection. I had so many demerits from Art's less than perfectly shined brass, boots, and wrinkled T-shirts that I had to write ten letters as punishment. Because I helped Art get through his inspection, I asked him to help me write my letters. He wrote about half of them, but it turned out that he used the wrong format, so I received more demerits for having him help me. We joked about that for a long time.

Once I graduated from Warrant Officer Cadet School (WOC-D), we started the actual Flight School Training program, the real reason we were all there. The whole class was split up: half of the class started academics in the morning, the other half started flight training in the morning. And after lunch, we would switch. We were also allowed to go home to live with our families for the duration of the course.

I was happy to be with my family but there was so much studying in flight school that I really didn't have time to enjoy any quality family time. Every waking moment was spent studying. Deonna was very tolerant of the situation and did what she could to make things easy on me. To help keep the house quiet, she would take the kids out to the park to play or take them with her when she had to go to the store. She even helped me study and often prepared my uniform for the next day.

Art graduated high in his class and seemed to be a natural pilot.

He flew like he had been born with wings. I graduated from Flight School just two weeks after Art.

After we graduated as pilots, Art went back to Sacramento to serve in his local National Guard unit, and I received my orders to the 25th Combat Aviation Battalion in the 25th Infantry Division in Hawaii. Deonna and I were both excited to go back to where we had been stationed ten years earlier.

Upon arrival to Hawaii and after signing into my new unit, I was asked if I wanted to take the additional two years for the accelerated promotion to Chief Warrant Officer Two (CW2). E-7's and above were given this opportunity.

I said, "Absolutely! I already have more than eleven years in and I plan to retire, so why not?"

That day I pinned on the new rank. Most of the others I went to school with graduated as Warrant Officer One (WO-1), which now put me two years senior to them. I was always a rank ahead of the rest of my graduating peers. Not long after I graduated and received my Chief Warrant Officer Two (CW2) rank, the regulation on early rank advancement changed, so it was only there long enough for me to take advantage of this unprecedented opportunity.

We were happy to do another tour of three years in Hawaii. The first Sunday back in Hawaii, we attended church at the same chapel where we had attended some ten years earlier as newlyweds. Deonna and I walked through the door and everyone jumped up and came over to us just like we had never left. I couldn't believe they remembered us after ten years.

Hawaii was a great place to be stationed for three more years. I liked my job as well as all the recreational things there were to do. I had several experiences while in Hawaii that were quite memorable. One of the most memorable was flying one of our new guys who had just arrived in our unit in Hawaii. It was my job to give Island Orientations to the new guys. We had just completed our flight around the Island and were headed back to Wheeler AFB where we kept the helicopters.

I decided on the way back that we would fly up through Pearl Harbor and over the Arizona Memorial. It was always a nice way to end your flight. As we flew back over the land mass only about ten miles from Wheeler AFB, I started to notice a vibration in the flight controls. I asked the new guy if he had noticed it as well, and he said yes. The rotor system started making a weird noise and the vibration started to get worse. The pilot in the other seat kept looking up at the rotor system, as if he was trying to see if something was wrong with it.

I told him, "It isn't going to do you any good to look up there; the rotor system is turning too fast to see anything."

He said, "Oh yeah, right." But he kept asking, "What's that noise?"

I said I didn't know for sure but I thought it was one of our rotor blades. I thought it didn't sound good, and the vibration was getting a little worse; but at the time, we were flying over a pineapple field, and I knew if I had to set it down, I would have to make a telephone call back to our Company. I was also hungry. We didn't have cell phones in those days.

I remembered a place that was just a little way from where we were at the time. It was a new fast food place called Jack in the Box, and it hadn't been there very long. Because I had to make a telephone call and I was hungry anyway, I landed in a pineapple field across the street from the Jack in the Box.

After I shut the helicopter down, I looked to see what the problem might have been. I immediately noticed that one of the rotor blades looked like it was coming apart and its trailing edge had separated about ten inches from the tip inward. The blade end cap was gone.

My copilot and I walked across the street and I went inside and made a telephone call back to the Company and told the Maintenance Test Pilot what had happened and where I was.

He just laughed and said, "Hang tight, bra (Hawaiian slang). I will jump in a helicopter and come see what's up."

After the call we went and bought burgers and waited for the test pilot to show up. We received a lot of attention from people driving by. Cars were backed up for at least a mile in both directions, and we weren't even blocking the road.

The news media came out as to be expected and wanted me to do an interview.

All I would say was the standard "no comment."

They asked if they could go up to the helicopter to take some pictures.

I said, "I don't think so."

The test pilot showed up about twenty minutes after I called him.

He looked the helicopter over, did some kind of quick temporary repair on the rotor blade and said, "You fly my helicopter back, bra. I will take this one in."

I said, "Okay," knowing I didn't want to fly the broken one back.

Later that day the Maintenance Test Pilot told me, "Bra you did the right thing landing when you did, because the rotor blades were separating, and had you flown a little bit longer, you would have probably lost control of the helicopter and crashed."

I loved my new job in aviation but really missed the atmosphere of being in a Special Operations Unit. While I was doing my tour in Hawaii as a pilot, I heard of a newly formed Special Operations Aviation Unit. They were hand-selecting pilots to be assigned to this special unit. The 160th SOAR is a highly trained Special Operations Army Aviation unit. It was right up my alley.

In 1986, I received orders for TF160 SOAR (Special Operations Aviation Regiment), referred to as TF160. My training in the Task Force came fast and furious. A couple of months into this rigorous training, I realized that as a new aviator I would need to gain more hours in night vision goggle flying in order to meet the demanding standards required of all Special Operations Aviators. Reluctantly, I left the Task Force to go to the 101st Airborne Division there at Ft. Campbell, Kentucky. For the next two and a half years I worked extremely hard to gain the experience required to be successful when I returned back to the TF160th. During that two and a half years with the 101st, I flew more night vision goggle hours than most pilots would get in five years.

I knew the high standards of the TF160, so I slowly raised the standard of the 101st, eventually becoming the Standardization Instructor Pilot for the whole unit. This did two important things for me: it always gave me the opportunity to continue my personal training so I could be accepted into TF160, and it made the 101st Aviation Regiment a much better unit.

At first, my attempts to raise the performance standards of the 101st pilots were met with a lot of resistance, even from one of the Company Commanders. Luckily for me the Battalion Commander, LTC Garrett, and my Company Commander, CPT Ron Buffkin, liked the new standards I had just set. I started giving goggle flight evaluation to all the other Flight Instructors first. Then all the instructors began to make sure their pilots in their individual companies were trained to the new standard. At first, there was some head butting, but when everyone got the hang of it, we became one of the best aviation units in the regular army.

My former commander, LTC Dick Cody, who is now a retired General, told me that the high standards that I had set prior to me going to TF160 played a huge part in their enormous victory during the Gulf War. That compliment was better than any award I could have ever received.

By the time these high standards were fully in place at the 101st Aviation Regiment, I had the flight time and experience to be accepted into the 160th SOAR, where I spent the rest of my career in B Company (Little Birds) TF160th.

CHAPTER SEVEN
Desert Storm

THE MEN I WORKED WITH in the TF160 were the best of the best. They were highly trained, self-motivated and very serious about their missions. There were no wimps in TF160 where very good men were frequently sent on life or death missions around the globe. Nobody did it for the fame or glamour, because nobody ever knew what went on inside these highly specialized operations.

The TF160 and other Special Operations operators were not under the direct command of the regular army. Even our personnel records were kept in a special section of the Department of the Army. The Special Operators I had come to know and love were a different breed of men on whom the government had come to rely on for those special missions across the globe. They were at the pinnacle of their military careers, with no higher station or honor available anywhere.

Special Operations guys didn't get transferred from one unit to another like regular army troops. Once you were in this position, you were there for the duration of your career, or until you were killed in the line of duty or asked to leave. The typical military protocol was somewhat relaxed. The guys I spent the next eleven years with, assigned to TF160, became brothers, extensions of my own family, and as equally loved as my own brothers. Even today, years after our time together, we continue to stay close. It was not unusual for me to be in Baghdad, Afghanistan, Amman Jordan, or any other place in the world, day or night, and get a phone call or visit from one of these brothers.

Our families received special instructions regarding the sensitive nature of our work from time to time. Wives and children were under the strictest confidentiality regulations. The children understood this and were very careful to avoid discussing anything about what their fathers did in the army.

When our unit was sent to the Gulf War in January 1991, it was never disclosed that we were even there. We conducted night missions very deep into Iraq and hit vital targets so the regular Army, Marines and Air Force could do their jobs during the day.

This was hard on the wives and children of the men in the unit. When everyone else was putting up yellow ribbons, our families had to tell their friends, neighbors and family that we were on a training exercise somewhere in the States. My daughter Jamie was in the ninth grade at the time. On one occasion, during church services, one of the adults who was in the army but didn't go to the Gulf War made a comment in front of everyone.

He said, "I know where your dad is right now."

Jamie was furious. She shouted, "You're going to get my dad killed!"

It created quite a scene in church. Because of the sensitive nature of our unit, Deonna was required to report the incident to the authorities. Subsequently, the guy received a visit from some nice men who encouraged him to refrain from making any further comments.

During Desert Storm, we were always aware of the possible scud attacks on U.S. forces. Because of the probability of chemical weapons being used, we were supposed to wear gas masks during scud attacks. We were all sleeping one night when a loud explosion rocked the building and sirens went off, indicating some kind of chemical attack. After I pulled myself up off the floor, I put on my gas mask and then jumped into my flight suit and slipped on my boots without tying them up.

The next thing I recall was the Task Force Commander, LTC Doug Brown, with excitement in his voice, saying "Launch the Little Birds! Go find them!"

I immediately ran out the door to the helicopter. When I got to the helicopter, the crew chief was there and had the helicopter ready to go. I jumped in the left seat, Lon Pearson jumping in the right seat, and started the helicopter up. It was so hot and hard to function with the gas mask on, so I took mine off and threw it out of the helicopter. The crew chiefs were yelling at me to put it back on.

One of them said, "Sir; no one said it was all clear yet; put your mask back on."

I told him "No, take that mask and get it out of my way! If I am going to die today, some of those bad guys are going with me!"

Looking back at it now, I know it was a dumb thing to do, but it really made me mad to have to wear that mask.

As we took off as a flight of two Little Birds, with Fred Horsley as the Flight Lead, we flew for a short time before we realized that there had been no scud attack on us. Rather, it was a friendly fire incident. Some knucklehead bomber pilot who didn't know there was a Special Operations unit that far north had an unused missile. His radar locked onto an airfield beacon at our forward operating base (FOB), assuming it was an enemy base. Without verifying the signal as friend or foe, he launched his missile at the beacon just prior to crossing the Iraqi-Saudi border. That missile came dangerously close to killing us. The next morning while on my early morning exercise run, I ran out to the destroyed airfield beacon and picked up a piece of the bomb. I still use it as a paperweight to remind me of one more close call.

After we had completed one of our missions deep into enemy territory we were on our way back when we received a call from the Tactical Operations Center (TOC) via the satellite radio, informing us that there was a storm building and that it was in our flight path heading back. Over in that part of the world, a dust storm can pop up very quickly with no warning at all. When a dust storm pops up like that, you literally cannot see ten feet in front of you and flying through it was out of the question.

As we were making our way back, we got within a half mile of our staging base (ARAR airfield) and could not see any sign of the base at all. The storm had arrived just minutes before our return. It was evident to us that we were not going to be able to make an approach into the airfield because we couldn't see it. About the time we thought we were right over the airfield we encountered more dust and clouds at our flight level and were beginning to lose site of each other.

In these circumstances, we had a briefed procedure just in case something like this happened. The weather condition was called Instrument Meteorological Conditions (IMC). When you were in a flight of more than one helicopter and you encountered these weather conditions, each helicopter had a predetermined heading to turn to and an altitude in which to climb to. Once the flight had executed the briefed plan, the procedure was supposed to keep each helicopter separated at a safe distance from each other vertically and laterally.

That night things didn't quite work out that way.

Our Flight Lead unexpectedly said over the radio, "I see a hole down there. I am descending."

It seemed everybody decided to do his own thing. Lon and I decided that we would continue our climb and try to recover to another airfield somewhere close. We found an airfield, Al Juf, approximately twenty miles south of the Iraq border and headed that direction.

While all this was going on, we heard on the SAT radio (Satellite Radio) that one of our Blackhawk helicopters was also on its way back from a rescue mission to pick up a wounded soldier. Even though there was a bad storm, the Blackhawk crew decided to try to make it back to our airfield because of the injured soldier. That was the last I heard on the radio, because I was landing at another airfield. The storm was so severe that radio communications were severely limited, and I was grounded for the night.

The next morning, I flew back to my base at ARAR airfield. There was helicopter wreckage scattered up and down the approach area about one hundred yards off the runway. The Blackhawk helicopter from the night before had crashed trying to make it back with the wounded Special Operations soldier, and all who were onboard were killed. Some of my buddies in the ground force thought that I had gone down too, because they hadn't heard from me all night. When I was landing at our base, I could see a couple of my buddies running to my helicopter. They were happy to see me after everything that happened that night.

When I came home from the Gulf War, I was awarded an Air medal for Valor. The award stated something about flying behind enemy lines to hit targets. I also received my Master Parachutist Wings, something that I was supposed to have received when I was in Special Forces but the paper work had been lost. Because I was on jump status in the Task Force and was Jump Master Qualified, I had the opportunity to make a few jumps. My paperwork for my Master Jump Wings was resubmitted and approved. General Downing pinned both awards on me at a ceremony held in front of the TF160 Headquarters.

My old buddies from the 101st Aviation Regiment, my old unit, didn't know we were in Iraq.

When they came home from Desert Storm they would say things like, "Man Dan, it's too bad you missed it. You wouldn't believe the kinds of things we did. You should've been there!"

All I could do was tell them how sorry I was to have missed out. I heard them brag about their missions for over a year until it was declassified that TF160 was there. Very few missions ever get declassified.

After I got home from the Gulf War, Deonna and I decided to take our family on a vacation to California to visit our families. Our plan was to have as much fun as we could because we didn't get to go to California that often to visit. My dad loved to camp and he had a boat, so we all headed out to Folsom Lake for a week of fun.

We were there about a week when I broke out in a rash over my entire body. We were camping so I thought I had been exposed to poison oak. I am extremely allergic to poison oak. My joints started swelling and I could not bend my fingers or any other joints. I went to the hospital at Mather AFB in Sacramento, and the doctor thought I had Lyme disease. They wanted to know where I had been and if I had been overseas recently. I could not tell them anything because the missions my Special Operations Aviation unit performed while in the Gulf War had not yet been declassified.

I gave the doctor the telephone number to my doctor at the TF160th and told them they would have to talk with him. They called the unit doctor and advised him of my symptoms. I didn't know what they discussed but after the conversation I was handed the telephone. The unit doctor at the TF160th told me to get back to Fort Campbell, Kentucky on the next flight. I told him I had driven and couldn't leave my family to drive back without me. He ordered a high dose of antibiotics and said to get back to Fort Campbell quickly.

I gave him the usual *"roger that"* and hung up the telephone.

I immediately went to my parents' house; we packed our things and drove off for Fort Campbell. On the way back we stopped in Salt Lake City, Utah, at the Clarks' house. They are friends we had known since being stationed in Hawaii the first time. Richard gave me a priesthood blessing that night in his home. We stayed the night and continued to Fort Campbell the next morning.

It usually took three and a half to four days to drive from Sacramento, California to Fort Campbell. Deonna had to do all the driving because I could not bend my knees. I sat in the back of the van with my legs all stretched out. I looked like the marshmallow man with my body all swollen up. That trip back to Fort Campbell was definitely no fun, to say the least, and it seemed to drag on forever.

The morning after I arrived back at Fort Campbell, the Task Force doctor met me at the hospital. They drew my blood and tested me several times for Lyme disease but it kept coming back negative. I had to take a blood test every six days for a couple of months. Each time they would draw my blood I would ask the doctors what caused those symptoms.

They replied, "We are not sure. We hope to know something soon."

They never did figure out what I had but I did get better. I attribute that to the high dose of antibiotics and the priesthood blessing I had received. I now think I had a reaction to something I was exposed to in Saudi during the Gulf War. Deonna was convinced I had Gulf War Syndrome and that it was cured because of early detection, antibiotics and a priesthood blessing. I guess we will never know for sure, but I give my thanks to God.

CHAPTER EIGHT
Mogadishu

OVER A PERIOD OF TIME the Special Ops community had been watching the outcome of the United Nations efforts in providing food and supplies to the people of Somalia. Warlord General Mohamed Farrah Aidid's militia was constantly impeding the United Nation's peacekeeping, humanitarian and resupply effort. His thug militia became more open and aggressive in their efforts to intercept and steal the humanitarian aid.

We monitored the situation as the U.S. military began taking a more active role with the humanitarian effort. But the United Nations soldiers began taking casualties and losing lives. In the spring of 1993, our Special Operations unit was alerted for a mission to Somalia. We went to Ft. Bragg, North Carolina rehearsing a mission with other Special Operations organizations. After we rehearsed this mission, for a couple of weeks and thought we would get the green light to conduct the mission, we were told to stand down.

The various Special Operations teams went back to home bases disappointed by the mission cancellation, but over the next couple of weeks the Somalia situation rapidly deteriorated. So once again, we were recalled back to Ft. Bragg to rehearse the mission.

Again after mission planning and rehearsal we were ordered to stand down. After we were back at Ft. Campbell for a couple of weeks, we received orders for a different mission and were deployed to Ft. Bliss, Texas where we planned and rehearsed for an entirely separate mission.

Not long after we arrived at Ft. Bliss, the situation flared up again in Somalia. Special Operations command had to put a new group of operators together to head back to Ft. Bragg for rehearsal of the same mission our group had already rehearsed twice before.

After a quick rehearsal, they were deployed to Mogadishu, Somalia. As soon as they touched down in Mogadishu, the Special Operations forces immediately began conducting missions to capture Warlord General Mohamed Farrah Aidid.

As declassified history shows, the mission had some disappointments. Although they did not capture the warlord, they were able to grab a few of his high-ranking men associated with his militia. On one of the relatively routine missions to capture Aidid, there was an ambush by hundreds of the warlord's militia. Eighteen men lost their lives and Mike Durant, a friend from TF160, was severely injured and taken as a prisoner after his Blackhawk helicopter was shot down.

After the news of our fallen comrades reached Ft. Campbell, my commander, Major Mark Brynick, sent me to Mogadishu to take over as the Little Bird Gunship Flight Lead. A few hours later I found myself aboard a C-5 Air Force Transport Airplane with an additional Little Bird Helicopter and a couple extra crewmembers. Aboard the

C-5 en route to Somalia were Special Ops Air and Ground Forces. The atmosphere aboard the C-5 was very somber but anxious to assist their fallen comrades and Special Ops buddies.

Our first stop was Cairo, Egypt where we thought it was just a refuel stop. After we off-loaded the airplane and moved to a holding tent, guys were getting a quick drink and bite to eat thinking we were leaving soon. After a long delay we found out that one of the C-5 pilots became ill and the flight crew was planning on going to a hotel for the night.

We were told that we were on the ground indefinitely. The Special Ops Ground Force Commander found out the reason for the delay and was very upset and ordered them to find us a replacement crew to get us to Somalia.

One of the Air Force crewmembers made some stupid remark like, "What's your big hurry? You guys will get there soon enough."

Our ground force commander took control of the situation and demanded that the Air Force crew get a pilot and get us off the ground immediately. He let them know we just had some of our guys killed and one taken prisoner. Another Air Force crew was assembled and we departed for Mogadishu. From the time we received the news of Mike Durant's helicopter being shot down to the time I arrived in Mogadishu, was less than forty-eight hours. That was how quickly our Special Operations unit was able to react to a situation on the other side of the world.

Many re-supply flights in and out of Mogadishu had received small arms fire at night, so we approached the Mogadishu International Airport from over the ocean in daylight hours to avoid small arms and mortar fire upon landing. Under cover of darkness the warlord's militia encircled the runway attempting to shoot down an American aircraft. Because it was sunset when we landed, we quickly turned around on the runway so the pilot could rapidly taxi to an off-load point on the runway. The crew needed to hot off-load and get back in the air before darkness fell. During a hot off-load, we unload the aircraft and equipment with all engines running on the C-5 for an immediate departure.

Usually the Air Force crew didn't help or get in our way when we were off-loading our stuff because we train to do it ourselves, but they were more than happy to help us this time so they could take off before it got dark. It seemed like it only took a few minutes to off-load the C-5. The Air Force wasted no time in taking off and heading back over the ocean for their return to Cairo.

I put all my gear in my assigned room and went to the TOC (Tactical Operations Center) to get a situation update, and then briefed the onsite Commander of the orders I had received from the B Company Commander MAJ Mark Brynick. I was sent to be the new B Company Flight Lead for all further operations and CPT Mark Jones would now be the B. Company OIC (Officer in Charge) while in country.

We were both welcomed, and then we received our situation up-date. As I walked out of the TOC I ran into my old friend, Gary Harrell, the Delta Commander. He and General Garrison, the Task Force Ranger Commander, were outside talking by the hangar when I approached them.

Gary asked me, "How was the flight?"

I replied, "Just glad to be here. I wanna find Mike."

We all knew Mike Durant and some of the guys who had been killed. There was a sense of urgency, and nobody had any desire to rest until we got Mike back and retrieved the bodies of friends who were still missing.

Gary Harrell said, "We'll talk later. You better run over to chow before they close and get a bite to eat. It might be a long night."

Gary was the guy who had retrieved my daughter's bike off the roof in Panama years earlier. He was a life-long friend.

I went to the mess hall and ate quickly, and then walked back toward the hangar. Gary Harrell, General Garrison and two other men were still outside by the hangar door discussing the situation, so I stopped to talk with them again. The sun had already set, and it had just begun to get dark.

A minute later, Captain Jones walked by and said, "Dan we're going to debrief a prior mission."

I said, "Roger, Sir, I'll be right there." I turned to General Garrison and Gary Harrell and the two other men and said, "I'll see you later tonight or in the morning."

General Garrison warned, "Be safe."

"Yes Sir General, you too."

I walked to the briefing room, only fifty feet away. As I entered the room, there was a very loud explosion and bright flash. My initial thought was *someone just had an accidental discharge with a hand grenade.* I quickly realized we had been hit with a mortar, something the bad guys did almost every night as the sunset.

I ran the few steps back to where I was talking with Gary Harrell and General Garrison. I found Gary lying on his back and General Garrison sitting on the ground. The two other men were also lying on the ground. One of them had an enormous head injury, and I believe he died two days later. The General's wounds were not as extensive, but I turned on my mini-mag flashlight and could see Gary Harrell was bleeding profusely from his leg.

As I knelt in a huge pool of blood from the four wounded men, I yelled, "We need a medic here!"

One of our new pilots, Warren Rogers, a former Air Force Paramedic (PJ), arrived quickly and went to work on Gary. Warren's quick action played a big part in saving Gary Harrell's life.

I was directed by the TOC as the Flight Lead to get the Little Birds airborne and see if we could find where the mortars came from. As the Little Bird Flight Lead, I quickly gathered the crews together and conducted a hasty brief on the mission. Only a few minutes after the mortar explosion, I had four Little Birds airborne.

We were circling the city to see any sign of a possible mortar position. We found two guys on a rooftop facing the airfield where the explosion had occurred. Every time I made a pass over them they would turn and face away from the airfield. I gave the controls to my copilot Paul White and had him fly toward them and slow the airspeed so I could see if they had any weapons on them. When we flew within fifty meters of them, I saw no weapons, but they immediately turned around and faced the other direction. I tried to get their attention to get them off the rooftop, but they just stood there.

I had Paul come back around so I could try to get them off the rooftop once more. As we passed them, I gestured for them to get off the rooftop by pointing vigorously to the ground, but once again, they did not move.

After we passed by them this time as a flight of four Little Birds, someone in the flight said "We are cleared hot," meaning shoot anyone on a rooftop.

I replied, "Negative!"

I instructed Paul to once again make a low pass by them. This time, my plan was to take my MP5 (a German-made compact assault weapon) I had bungeed to my chest and point it at them to show them I was serious this time, and fire a burst of rounds to get their attention if needed.

This time, Paul flew lower and slower to within a few feet of them. As we approached I grabbed my MP5 and pointed it right at them. When they saw the MP5 pointed at them, they had a look of panic and despair on their faces. They turned and jumped off the roof. The rest of the flight we spent flying and looking for any indications of where Mike Durant could be.

When we landed and conducted the mission debrief, one of the pilots asked me why I did not shoot the guys on the rooftop.

I replied with a question. "Did anyone see a weapon of any kind in their hands?"

They answered, "No, but we are cleared hot for anyone on a rooftop after nightfall."

My answer to all of them was, "I am the Flight Lead and the chain of command has put a lot of faith and trust in me. And they expect me to make the right decision however unpopular it might be."

Everyone was under a lot of stress. We had one guy captured, eighteen others killed a couple days before, and another two guys seriously wounded only minutes before. It was easy for us to get angry and trigger-happy.

I was the Flight Lead, and that makes me the decision-making guy in the air. Our rules of engagement were clear, and the rules allowed us to kill the two men on the roof. It was not the first time I had been in that kind of situation; but in this instance I had to make a hard decision, under emotional circumstances, and I chose to avoid firing. In the heat of the moment, some of the crewmembers in the four helicopters may have sought revenge rather than self-defense and justice. Under the circumstances, I understood their feelings and even had to keep my own feelings in check.

I continued, "The decisions we make in combat are decisions we live with for the rest of our lives. The two guys on that rooftop didn't pose any immediate threat to us, and that's the reason I did not take their lives."

I believe the decision I made that night was the right one, and the other guys reluctantly agreed. The next morning, I walked past the scene of the mortar explosion from the night before. The mortar round hit exactly where I was standing while talking to Gary and the other wounded men.

That night I wrote in my journal, "It is time for me to retire, too many close calls."

The rest of my time in Somalia was spent doing nightly missions we referred to as "Eyes over the Mog." I was the Flight Lead for the rest of our Little Bird missions. We did one rehearsal mission, anticipating a rescue recovery of Mike Durant, if we would have received creditable intelligence on his location.

Mike was released about ten days after he was taken as a POW. There was an overwhelming excitement and relief when we received the news of his release. Mike did not spend much time with us because of his injuries; he was immediately put on a C-141 Air Force transport to start his journey back to the United States with a medical stop in Germany. With the C-141 on the taxiway awaiting Mike's arrival, everyone in Task Force Ranger was out at the flight line to see him off.

Our Special Operations group headed home soon after Mike's release from captivity. The reception upon landing at Fort Campbell, Kentucky was one to remember. As we de-boarded the airplane, Lee Greenwood was singing his famous song *"God Bless the USA."* Deonna and the kids were all there to meet me, and I was thankful to be home again.

Special Operations Units didn't usually have a reception of this magnitude when they returned from a real mission. But with the circumstances surrounding the shoot-down of Mike Durant, the unit's mission and location was all over the news. It was a very nice reception but it was Sunday, and Deonna and I felt it was important to attend church. We spent a minimal amount of time at the reception and then left and went to church. We didn't even go home first so I could change into a suit. I walked into the chapel dressed in my desert uniform.

We belonged to a military congregation or ward, so it was not really unusual for someone to show up to church in an army uniform. Even though it was not spoken, everyone knew where I had been and welcomed me home.

CHAPTER NINE
Events Leading To The Accident

LESS THAN A YEAR AFTER returning from Mogadishu I experience the ultimate life-changing event of my life thus far. My helicopter accident was something that stayed with me in the back of my mind every day of my life, and I didn't go a day without thinking about the day that had changed my life so drastically and forever. It was a day that brought so much emotional pain that I felt I couldn't bear it. It was a day that brought so much physical pain that it sometimes seemed as though it would never end. It was a day that taught me what I was made of. I would not want to go through it again, but in an unexplainable way, I was thankful for the lessons learned on that day and for months, maybe years afterward. I have a much deeper understanding of God's love and the spiritual aspect of life and how important faith and obedience to God's commandments were. I understood the purpose of life just a little better than before.

I just hoped I could live up to the expectations God had of me and be worthy of His tremendous love.

I loved Carlos like a brother, and I still miss him. Carlos was a very dear friend who was killed on a hot July evening in 1994. I was with him when he died.

Twenty-two years after I had joined the army, I had planned to retire. My work in Special Operations had taken a lot of my time away from my family. Deonna and I discussed retirement and mutually agreed it was time. Our two oldest children were grown and away from home, but we still had three teenagers at home.

With the decision made to retire, I began processing the paperwork to leave the army. It was a bittersweet feeling, because the army had been my home for so long and I felt good about the work I had done for my country. Not wanting to leave Special Operations completely, I took a job working as a Civilian Military Instructor (CMI) for the Task Force 160th. These jobs required you to be a former Flight Lead and Instructor Pilot in the unit to qualify.

In May of 1994, I started working as a CMI and was on transitional leave from the army. This meant that I was still technically in the army but using my final vacation days and still receiving all active duty benefits and pay while I was working my new civilian job. I was scheduled to officially retire from the army on September 30, 1994.

On July 19, 1994, my former boss, Major Mark Brynick told me he needed to talk to me and asked for me to come to his office the first chance I got. I wasn't sure what he wanted, and I kept going over in my mind all the things I had done or said recently that he might want to talk with me about. I knew I wasn't being promoted because I was on terminal leave and getting ready to retire from the army on September 30th. Usually when you got called in the commander's office, it was not for a pat on the back, so I was preparing myself for the worst. Major Brynick was one of the best commanders I had ever had, and I admired and respected him. I walked into his office and anxiously waited for what he had to say.

He began by saying, "You know you are not out of the army yet."

I said, "Yes, sir."

I immediately knew where he was going with this. The problems in Haiti were flaring up, and I had heard rumors of the unit going there.

He said, "You know we are short Flight Leads and I could legally call you back to do this mission. I've been asked to see if you are willing to deploy with us if we need you."

The Major had the authority to call me back on active duty, but he didn't need to.

I replied, "That's okay. I don't want to miss a shooting match anyway. Tell the big boss I'm ready to go."

He grinned and said, "I already did, because I knew what your answer would be."

I replied, "Roger that, sir."

He reached out to shake my hand and told me, "Go to the range tomorrow and get current again. Be packed and ready to go on a moment's notice."

And with that, my retirement was put on hold for one more mission. It was a fateful decision that would cause a lot of pain and grief to a lot of people.

I had a friendly relationship with Major Brynick and we stood and talked a bit longer before I left his office. I didn't have any bad feelings about going. I just didn't know what I was going to tell Deonna and how she was going to take it.

Like most military wives, Deonna had put up with a lot. For more than twenty years I was frequently away from home in dangerous circumstances, and that took a toll on her. With my being on terminal leave, she finally felt like I was safe and that our army life was finally over. We both just wanted to lead a normal life outside the army.

On the evening of July 19th, I went home to try to explain the situation to Deonna. After dinner, we sat down so I could tell her what had happened.

I said, "I need to go to the range tomorrow and get current on shooting."

Deonna had a surprised look and said, "But, you're a civilian instructor now; you're not supposed to be going to the range anymore."

I could see the concern on her face, and there was no easy way to say it.

"Major Brynick needs a Flight Lead for another mission and I agreed to go."

Deonna said, "I have a bad feeling about this Danny. I can't believe this is happening. You are supposed to be retiring and our lives in the army were supposed to be over. I finally felt like you were going to be safe and that I didn't have to worry so much about you."

I knew my words wouldn't make her feel any better, but I could only say, "I'm sorry. There's a mission being planned to Haiti and they need me. Technically, I'm still in the army."

"I know, but haven't you done enough?" she said. Deonna sat stoically feeling disheartened, but knew there was nothing she could do about it.

I tried to ease her disappointment. "As soon as this mission is over, I'll be home and we'll continue the plan to retire. The mission will only last a few days."

You Have To Live Hard To Be Hard

Deonna lifted her head and looked into my eyes. "But you promised!" Deonna did what she had always done; she supported me and said what she always said before every mission, "Don't forget how much I love you."

We had been married for twenty-two years and had learned to put things in the Lord's hands, trusting Him with everything. I knew Deonna prayed every night for my safety, especially when I was away on missions. I had heard her pray many times for my protection, asking the Lord to bring me home safely. In her daily prayers, she reminded the good Lord how much she needed me and loved me. It felt good to know that my loving, faithful wife was praying for my safety.

The next day, Deonna went to work knowing I would be flying and shooting at the range that night. I assured her I would be safe, and would be home early. Normally, when we went to the range, we wouldn't be home until three or four in the morning after long hours of night training, but I didn't plan to be late and told her I would be home by ten o'clock that night.

Because I was planning to retire, I had not recently been to the shooting range and needed to get current in shooting again. Helicopter pilots in TF160 train for thousands of hours, shooting with such accuracy that it is termed "surgical shooting." As Special Operations pilots, we each fired more rounds than the entire regular Army Attack Battalion and Air Cavalry Division at Fort Campbell, Kentucky, fired in a whole year.

It took that much practice to gain the kind of accuracy required for all of our missions. For example, on one mission, I had six U.S. Navy SEALS on the ground seeking a target. The SEALS were within seventy-five feet of the target. When you would shoot this close to friendly forces it is referred to as a "danger-close" mission. It was at night, and I was wearing night vision goggles. I was a thousand yards out flying in an orbit, waiting for the SEALS to give me the go-ahead. At their direction, I flew inbound, locked onto the target, and fired a burst of machine gun rounds. Any stray rounds would put the SEALS in danger, but all rounds hit the target.

Shooting danger-close missions in very close proximity to ground Special Ops guys was a particularly high-stress maneuver. Flight Leads made critical combat decisions under extremely difficult circumstances, with no time to ponder and discuss the options. Decisions in these circumstances had to be made instantly. Friendly fire incidents were the worst thing that could happen so we took our jobs very seriously.

Sometimes our missions seem impossible and too risky. Often, in briefings with high-ranking officials who could not comprehend our very precise capabilities, we were asked, "Are you sure you can do this?"

When we fired from a helicopter platform, with the vibrations and movement of the bird, it was very difficult to become a surgical shooter, and being away from the bird for only a couple of weeks was enough to dull your accuracy. With a mission to Haiti in only a couple of days, it was necessary to do some practice runs and freshen up my skills.

The next day at the flight line, I was supposed to fly with Larry Kulsrud to the range but he later came to me and said he couldn't fly with me and that he wasn't feeling well. I thought it was kind of out of the norm but brushed it off and started looking for someone else to fly with. I then asked Jay Johnson to go flying with me. He was initially excited about it and agreed. A little later he came to me and said he couldn't fly because he wasn't feeling well.

I thought, *Man! Something must be going around making everyone sick.*

Well, I wouldn't give up so I called Jamie Weeks who was at home and asked him to fly with me. He told me he had just opened a beer and drank some so that disqualified him as well. Most guys would give their eyeteeth to fly and shoot at the range. It was a coveted opportunity, so it was very unusual for so many guys to decline the chance to fly. I was getting frustrated but really needed to fly, so I went over to A Company, the other Little Bird Company, and found a guy who needed a night vision goggle evaluation and told him that I would give him the evaluation if he flew with me to the range that evening. He agreed.

Deonna went to work but had an uncomfortable feeling all day and felt compelled to call me on my pager over and over during the day to tell me to be careful. She said, "Are you sure you have to go to the range today?"

"Yes, Deonna, I am sure. Don't worry. I'll be home by ten."

She always ended the conversation by saying, "Just be careful and remember I love you."

This same conversation occurred at least seven times that day. I should have listened I guess, but I was so concerned about getting current for this mission that I was too stubborn to pay attention to the warnings. I knew there was something that had to be done and nothing was going to stop me from doing it, even if I had to fly alone.

Major Brynick's words rang clear in my mind, "Be ready to go on a moment's notice."

Well, the guy from A Company did fly with me to the range late that afternoon and everything went well. After we landed at the range and shut down the helicopter, I walked to the bleachers, awaiting the safety briefing for the night shooting exercises. When I got there, my good friend Carlos Guerrero was there with the rest of the guys waiting for the range safety briefing.

He had just completed his daytime portion of the range and was waiting for the night portion.

Because I was only going to shoot one load of rockets and be done before they started the night range, I asked Carlos, "Hey, Carlos, I have to get current and need to shoot a load of rockets, do you want to fly with me? This could be our last time to fly together since I am retiring."

Carlos replied, "Okay, Dano. As long as you don't get mad because I shoot better than you!"

We both laughed. We were always kidding each other this way. Carlos and I had been on many missions together and were very close friends. On May 5th of every year, as a joke we both wore T-shirts that had *Cinco de Mayo* on them. We would joke with everyone, telling them we were taking the day off, because it was Mexican Independence Day.

I got to know Carlos's parents, and they would bring me Mexican breads when they came to visit Carlos from their home in Texas. Carlos would come to our home, and our kids really liked him. Our daughter Jamie, who was a young teenager at the time, liked to argue with him. She didn't like guys to tell her she couldn't do something because she was a girl. I guess she was a little like me. She would do everything in her power to show she could do things as well as any guy could do them. Carlos loved to tease her about it and would go out of his way to say something to get her going.

Carlos was proud of the fact that he was an Army Ranger. It was a badge of honor to him, but Jamie, used to tease him. "Rangers aren't that tough! Even a teenage girl could be a Ranger!"

Carlos would cry out, "There's no way a girl could pass Ranger school!"

Jamie always argued back, "Well, I'm gonna prove you wrong. I'll be the first female Ranger!"

Carlos had a great relationship with all my kids. He was family. Sometimes Carlos would joke around in a way that would offend someone if he or she didn't know him well. Our oldest daughter, Michelle, was dating Mike Quinlan, whom she later married. One day, Michelle and Mike were outside by the front door when Carlos came over. They had just started dating, so Carlos didn't know Mike.

As Carlos approached the house, he said, "Hey, Michelle! Who's the dork?"

Needless to say, Mike was offended, so we had to explain to Mike that Carlos jokes around that way and didn't intend to offend him.

Well, that evening started pretty normal. We had a range safety briefing before we flew. Carlos and I headed toward the helicopter. I sat in the left seat, and Carlos sat in the right. The helicopter could be controlled from either seat. Because of the amount of fuel I had onboard, we could only take six rockets. We planned to do only six passes, shooting mini-gun and one rocket per pass. A mini-gun was a Gatling gun that fires 7.62mm rounds at the rate of four thousand rounds per minute. We had two of those guns onboard, so there was a massive amount of firepower with both guns firing.

I flew the first three passes and then handed the controls over to Carlos for the fourth pass. With each pass we would bump up and shoot the target with a mini-gun and fire one rocket. Then we would bank hard right and go around and do another pass. Carlos had a direct hit and I took the controls from him for the fifth pass. I also had a direct hit and bragged about it. We both laughed and were having a good time. I told Carlos he could take the last pass and then we would land and I would go home.

Carlos was making his final run at the target, an old army tank. As he fired the mini-guns and a rocket, he had a direct hit, but there was an unusual explosion like I have never seen before.

Shrapnel came right at us and I lifted my left arm to cover my face, shouting to Carlos, "I think we're going to be hit with something."

We flew without doors, so shrapnel could easily hit us directly. Carlos banked hard right but at that moment, we had a compressor stall and the engine hesitated momentarily, which caused the helicopter to lose power. Carlos tried but could not pull the aircraft up.

CHAPTER TEN
The Accident

WHAT HAPPENED NEXT IS PAINFULLY difficult to describe. We hit the ground very fast and very hard. The safety board estimated the initial impact was eight times the force of gravity. We bounced, end over end, for more than a hundred meters. The helicopter burst into flames. During the first impact we bounced high enough to clear a fifteen-foot tree, burning the top of the tree as we soared over it.

I remember hearing an eerie crackling sound as my legs and ribs were being broken with each impact. A couple of the rotor blades and the tail boom broke away as we tumbled down the range. Both fuel tanks on the helicopter burst open and were spewing fuel on us as we tumbled.

As we came to a rest with the helicopter on its right side, flames engulfed the cockpit. Carlos was pinned in his seat. I was dazed, strapped into my seat by a harness, and was surprised to hear the noise of the still-running engine. With a couple of rotor blades gone, the engine began winding up getting extremely loud.

Everything happened so quickly. Dazed and trying to regain my senses, I heard Carlos screaming for help and the mini-gun ammunition rounds exploding in the fire.

Suddenly, everything became very quiet and an unexplained calmness came over me. It was the most peaceful quiet I have ever experienced. There was no place on Earth where it was that quiet. You could always hear your heartbeat, a bird chirping, the wind rustling, something! But I heard nothing at all.

At that moment I heard a voice say, "Undo your seatbelt, and you will be free." The voice was very distinct and explicit, very peaceful and comforting, but a voice I have never heard before.

A moment later all the deafening sounds of the helicopter, the flames, the rounds cooking off, and Carlos's screams for help returned. My mind was reeling, but I didn't question what I had heard. I just knew that if I could get free, I could help Carlos get free as well. With my right hand, I reached down through the fire toward Carlos to release his seatbelt, but the heat from the fire was so intense. I did this about three times and finally caught hold of his seatbelt and pulled his and then mine about the same time.

Because of the position of the helicopter lying on its right side, my left seat was positioned above, and Carlos's was below. When I pulled my seatbelt, I should have fallen toward Carlos, but I didn't. All I knew was that after I pulled my seatbelt release, I opened my eyes and saw the stars in the sky and the helicopter burning about ten meters to my left. I didn't know how I had gotten out of the helicopter; I just knew I didn't do it myself.

I didn't know it at the time, but both of my legs were badly broken, and bones were protruding through my left leg. My left leg was broken in five places, and my right ankle was completely severed. My broken ribs had punctured my lungs. As I lay on the ground, momentarily stunned at how I was safely removed from the wreckage, my thoughts quickly turned to Carlos.

I sat up, and both my legs were in cockeyed positions. I grabbed the legs of my flight suit and flung my legs one at a time in front of me in a straight position. My right boot was still on fire and I swung my flight gloves and tried to beat out the fire. It would go out for a second and then reignite. The sleeve on my right arm was ripped to the elbow and the flesh on my arm was burning. I started to use my left hand to put the flame out but realized it would burn my hand so I swung my burning arm up and down fast and hard, and the burning skin fell off causing the weeds next to me to catch on fire. It was the end of July, so the terrain was dry, and the brush caught fire easily.

I struggled to stop the ground fire around me but could hear Carlos's voice over the deafening sound of the engine, screaming, my name, "Dano, help me!"

He was still in the helicopter, and I later learned that part of his body was pinned under the wreckage, so even after I released his harness, he was unable to escape. I tried to tell him I was coming but I could not speak above a whisper. I hate remembering the terrible screams of my friend, but I've never been able to erase the sounds from my memory. They remain there in a dark and ugly place with other sounds and images from my military career.

I did not know it then, but my broken ribs had punctured my lungs and they were filling with blood. I was struggling to breathe, but I thought my breathing problem was from panic.

I was ashamed of myself for what I believed was panic, and I thought; *now this is pretty chicken of me. Here I am safe, outside of the helicopter, and my best friend is inside burning to death. And I am too panic-stricken to help him.*

I couldn't speak loudly enough for Carlos to hear me over the sounds of the flames, the whining engine, and the bullets cooking off. Not knowing my lungs were filling with blood, I thought my weak voice was because of fear or panic. It was an awful feeling.

Carlos kept calling for me, and I kept trying to get to him. I tried to stand up, but a bone tore through my left leg. With both legs broken, I fell back down and realized my upper body was intact. So while I was lying down, I tried to use my shoulders and rear end to crawl toward Carlos. I had only moved a few inches when my shoulder hit a small tree, and I was too badly incapacitated to go any farther.

Just then the helicopter exploded, and Carlos's voice went silent. As I kept trying to crawl to the helicopter on my back and I could see his body slumped over. I suspected Carlos was probably dead, but I was not willing to accept that. I continued trying to inch my way toward him.

Charlie Weigandt was the designated Flight Lead for the day and night gunnery training and had just witnessed the crash from the bleachers. He immediately ran to his helicopter and flew to the crash site, hoping to locate survivors. After he reviewed the scene from the night sky, Charlie made a radio call to the Range Control Officer, Ricky Thornton.

"Range Control, the crash was catastrophic. Nobody could have survived."

Back at the re-arm pad near the bleachers, they immediately mobilized a rescue crew. Two TF160 medics raced toward the burning helicopter in a Humvee. It took four and a half minutes for them to make their way to the crash site, arriving moments after the large explosion that silenced Carlos.

The terrain was rough, and the brush was thick, so they could not drive all the way to the wreckage. Instead, they stopped the Humvee and grabbed a stretcher and ran to where the fuselage of the helicopter lay burning. When the medics approached the devastation, they did not expect to find any survivors.

In the light of the fire, I noticed one of the medics moving quickly toward me, and I was surprised and frustrated to have him throw his body on top of mine. I was having difficulty breathing, so I tried to throw him off of me, but he kept getting back on top of me.

Frustrated with him, I kept asking myself, *why is he doing this?*

In my efforts to help Carlos, and stop myself from burning, I had forgotten the danger of the exploding bullets. This TF160 medic was doing what he was trained to do, placing himself in harm's way to shield my body from the bullets going off in all directions, preferring to have the bullets strike his own body rather than the body of his patient. I was honored to be able to work with the caliber of men I work with. You will never find better men.

The other medic was trying to place a neck brace on me, but I took it off and threw it away, doing my best to holler at him, "I can't breathe! I don't need that."

My words came out as mere whispers. I repeatedly told them, "Help Carlos! Help him! I tried to save him! Please help him!"

The medics had already determined that Carlos was dead, so they ignored my plea and continued to work on me. They cut off my flight gear and my flight suit and attempted to cut off my long white underwear and undershirt.

Some people know that Mormons wear undergarments with special religious meaning. In the Mormon Temples, we promise to always wear the special garments and live pure and honest lives to the very best of our ability. In return we are promised that the garments will be a special protection, both physically and spiritually. I took my religious commitments seriously. These garments were sacred to me, so when the medics tried to cut them off, I tried to stop them. There was a short scuffle between us, but in the end, they succeeded in cutting away my underclothing and discovered that there were no burns on my skin in any place covered by my garments. Having no burns on any area covered by the garments had certainly saved my life.

Minutes after the crash, a Medevac helicopter was requested by the Range 29 Safety Officer Ricky Thornton. In one of the many miracles of my life, it turned out that a fully staffed Medevac helicopter crew was already in the air nearby on a training mission. That helicopter crew was immediately dispatched to the crash site.

About the time the medics were putting me on the stretcher, the Medevac helicopter was overhead looking for a spot to land.

The pilot made a radio call to the medics on the ground. "I've got you in sight. You can stop shooting off pin flares."

One of the medics responded with a handheld radio, "Nobody is firing flares. Those are tracer rounds cooking off."

The pilot, concerned about the stray bullets, did an immediate climb and landed about a hundred meters away from the crash site. The medics had to carry me on a stretcher away from the crash site. This was very painful, and each step caused me to moan with pain. They fought their way through all the brush and onto a dirt road to the Humvee and then carefully loaded me and drove to where the helicopter had landed about three hundred meters away.

Once the Medevac helicopter landed, the flight medics wanted to perform another assessment of my condition. The TF160 medics had already done this, and they knew time was extremely critical, so they wanted me loaded immediately.

One of the TF160 medics hollered, "We already assessed him. Just get him loaded and to the hospital!"

The flight medic hollered back, "We can't do that. We have to check him before we load."

The bantering between the two groups of medics continued for a few seconds, both groups of medics wanting to do the right thing. But the TF160 medics were right. Time was too critical for a new set of medics to waste time on a second assessment.

With a weak voice, I tried to get things moving. "I don't care what we do. Let's just do something!"

After I said that, one of my medics reached up and pulled the flight medic off the helicopter and threw him on the ground. My medics carefully loaded me, jumped aboard the helicopter, and then yelled to the pilot, "Let's fly!"

We lifted off, but my breathing was becoming increasingly difficult. I tried to breathe slowly and calm myself but still didn't realize I was drowning in my own blood from punctured lungs.

Disappointed in myself, I thought, *Come on, Dan. Don't panic. Just breathe slowly.*

While in flight to Blanchfield Army Community Hospital at Ft. Campbell, the intensity of pain continually increased.

I remember telling the medics, "I'm on fire!"

"Sir, you're not on fire."

I kept insisting I was on fire, so one of the medics lifted the sheet to prove there were no flames. I laid back and began to fade in and out of consciousness, feeling myself slipping away.

When they offloaded me from the helicopter and started to roll me into the Emergency Room, I pulled the medic by his collar down close to my face and said, "Paul, call my wife and tell her to call the Bishop and get here as fast as they can."

Paul didn't understand and kept insisting I would be all right and that I didn't need the Bishop. I grabbed him again with the last bit of strength I had left and pulled him close to me.

I repeated, "Call my wife and tell her to call the Bishop."

He saw the desperate look on my face and said, "Okay, sir. I'll do it."

Deonna had gone home from work at 4:00 PM and was still feeling uncommonly nervous. She had a church meeting that started at 7:30 PM that normally lasted until 9:00 PM, but by 8:15, the same moment Carlos and I crashed, she just couldn't sit any longer and left her church meeting and went home.

When she answered the phone at 8:45 PM, she instinctively knew something was wrong, and had known it all day. Against protocol, this medic made the call to my wife about a half hour after the accident.

Deonna answered the phone, "Hello?"

"This is Paul Stevenson; I am a medic from your husband's unit."

Her stomach turned, but she said, "Is everything okay?"

Paul was concerned about alarming her as to how serious it was. He simply said, "There's been an accident on Range 29. Dan's hurt, and he's in the Emergency Room at Blanchfield. He asked that you call the Bishop and come to the hospital as quick as you can."

A Bishop was the religious leader of Mormon congregations known as wards. I wanted Bishop Flake, a close friend, at my side to give me a blessing.

Deonna thought that because I was alive and talking that I must not have been hurt that badly. There had been a few helicopter accidents in our unit over the years. Most of them were relatively minor and caused back injuries or head injuries but no burns or deaths. She hoped it was not serious.

Our daughter Jamie called Bishop Flake while Deonna scrambled to get herself and the kids dressed to go to the hospital.

Deonna called her good friend Debbie Bowyer. "Debbie, it's me. Danny's been hurt in an accident. Can you meet me at the hospital?"

Debbie's voice showed concern. She answered, "Of course, I'll be right there."

We had five children. Our oldest son, Chris, was a helicopter crew chief in D Company, and was out of town with the TF160[th] on a training mission. Our oldest daughter, Michelle, was married to Mike Quinlan, who was also assigned to TF160[th] and lived just a few miles away. Jamie, the oldest of our kids still living at home, called Mike and Michelle and they also drove to the hospital.

Deonna, Jamie, and our two younger sons, Jason and Art, ages fifteen and thirteen, jumped into the van and drove to the hospital, which was only about half a mile down the road from our house.

Our Special Operations unit had their own psychiatrist, Dr. Franklin, constantly on staff. In any emergency situation like this, his job was to stay close to the family members to make sure no sensitive information was leaked, as well as take care of the needs of the family. Dr. Franklin followed Deonna everywhere she went and monitored everything she said.

When Deonna was finally called to talk with the ER doctor, Dr. Franklin stayed at her side. The ER doctor rattled off all my injuries, but Deonna wasn't registering what he was telling her. To her, broken legs and burns didn't sound that bad.

She asked, "Does he have a back injury?"

The doctor gave her a puzzled look and said, "No."

"Does he have a head injury?" she asked.

Again the doctor looked at her like she was crazy and said, "No."

Then she asked, "Was there another pilot in the helicopter?"

The ER doctor blurted out, "Yes, he died."

At that moment Deonna realized the accident was serious.

Dr. Franklin immediately said to the ER Doctor, "You aren't supposed to tell anyone that."

Deonna ran out of the room crying, Dr. Franklin right behind her. As she tried to regain her composure, gasping and breathing deeply, holding back the sobs, Deonna looked out across the dark parking lot and saw Debbie Bowyer hurrying toward the Emergency Room. Deonna ran toward her and they embraced, Dr. Franklin close behind.

Deonna knew Dr. Franklin was nearby, so while they were still embracing, she quietly whispered in Debbie's ear, "Somebody died, Debbie."

Debbie didn't realize it had been a helicopter accident and struggled to process the information. She initially thought it had been an auto accident or something.

Debbie's husband was also in TF160 and they lived two doors down from us, so she understood the sensitivity of the situation. The two weeping women walked back into the hospital and sat with the kids in the waiting room.

Deonna told the kids that there was another pilot in the helicopter but she didn't know who it was. She didn't tell them the other pilot had been killed.

The kids kept asking, "Who was the other pilot? When is his family going to come to the hospital?"

With Dr. Franklin still monitoring the family, she was unable to discuss the very few details she knew. She could only say, "I don't know."

The kids continued asking, "When will they bring the other pilot to the hospital? Where is the other pilot's family?"

I was not sure how much time passed before Deonna was finally allowed to see me. As she walked down the long hallway toward my room, she saw me lying on the examining table.

I was repeating over and over again, "Doc, I tried to get Carlos out of the helicopter but I couldn't."

The doctor ignored me as he hustled around the room adjusting monitors and medical devices. Although I don't remember anything, Deonna later told me that my head kept following the doctor's movements around the room as I kept repeating the same thing over and over again, "Doc, I tried to get Carlos out of the helicopter but I couldn't."

Deonna, now realizing that the pilot who was killed was our dearest friend, Carlos Guerrero, came to my bedside and stood by me, but was at a loss for words. She touched my hand, tears running down her cheeks, and whispered, "Oh, Danny."

Blanchfield Army Community Hospital was an army hospital with military doctors and staff. They had been briefed on the sensitivity of the situation, so when the doctor realized Deonna had learned the identity of the dead pilot, this same doctor, who was chastised for telling her that the other pilot had died, asked, "Who let you come back here? You need to go back to the waiting room right now!"

Deonna was shocked because a nurse had told her that she could see him now. The ER Doctor whisked her out of the room and back to the waiting room. Even though she knew who the other pilot was and that he had been killed, she understood that she could not repeat that information to anyone, even our kids. As a longtime wife of a Special Operations soldier, she knew the drill.

Bishop Flake arrived with Brother Airhart and Brother Luciano from our ward. Mormons called each other brother and sister to emphasize that we were all God's children. The Bishop asked the ER Doctor if they could be allowed a minute to come to my bedside and give me a blessing. I was in extreme pain but when Bishop Flake put his hands on my head I felt as if all my troubles had vanished and I was floating in the air with no pain at all. I don't recall the words of the blessing Bishop Flake gave me but I heard him say, "Amen."

That was when I was able to relax and went unconscious. My mind was relieved and I knew everything would be okay. I will be forever grateful for what Bishop Flake did for me that night. He was a spiritual giant and an honorable man.

As I was wheeled down the hall to the operating room, I was groaning and barely conscious but heard the kids say, "Dad, we love you. We will be here when you come out of the operating room."

The last words I recall were from my tearful wife, Deonna, "I love you, Danny. We're here for you."

Paul Stevenson, one of the TF160 medics, came to the hospital to see Deonna. Paul is the medic who called Deonna. Paul's face was bright red and he looked as if he had gotten a 2nd degree sunburn. Deonna asked him about it. He told her that he and the other medic were both burned by the intense heat from the helicopter fire while they were treating me.

Deonna was given a plastic bag containing my clothes and belongings. When she opened it to retrieve my wallet and watch, she immediately closed the bag. The smell of JP4, the helicopter fuel was so strong it took her breath away.

Deonna also had to make a very dreaded phone call to my parents. She spoke with my mom and told her I had been in a helicopter accident but I would be all right. Mom and Dad wanted to come right away, but Deonna said to wait, because she wasn't sure where or when they would transfer me to another hospital.

It was around five o'clock in the morning when Dr. Franklin came in to see the family. They were sitting in the waiting room hoping for news about my condition. The doctor had finally received permission to release the name of the other pilot, and that was when the kids first learned that our close family friend had been killed. All the kids broke down at the dreadful news. On top of losing a dear friend, they were angry that they had been lied to. It was hard for Deonna to watch the kids as they realized Carlos was dead. Not only was their dad in serious condition but even worse, Carlos was gone.

About 5:15 AM I finally came out of surgery and was put in the intensive care unit. A wonderful surgeon named Dr. Kevin James came out and gave Deonna a rundown on my injuries. She was told I had five spiral breaks to my left leg and the right leg was broken in half at the ankle. Because of the burns they couldn't cast my right leg and he had to put a metal plate in to support my ankle. My ribs were broken and had punctured my lungs and I had third and fourth-degree full thickness burns to my right leg and 3rd degree burns to my right arm. I had severe burns to 31 percent of my body. Deonna was no expert on burns so she didn't realize the severity of the situation. She had no idea what a full thickness burn was and didn't know to ask. She only knew that burns were often fatal because of infection and loss of fluids.

Everything seemed to be happening so fast, and everything just became a blur to Deonna. She said she didn't remember who it was, but someone in the unit came to her and tried to convince her to sign papers to have me medically retired. Deonna knew that the medical attention I would receive after I was retired would not be nearly as good as if I were on active duty, so she said, "No, stop his retirement and put him back on active duty."

He tried to reason with her, but she was insistent. They did what she asked, so I was placed back on active duty. She could be sure we would have income while I was recovering as well. I found out months later that the reason they tried to get her to medically retire me was because they didn't think I would live through the night, and by medically retiring me, it would give Deonna and the kids much better survivor benefits than if I had died on active duty.

An hour later, Deonna was back at home but unable to sleep. It was 6:00 AM. She kept thinking of our dear friend, Suzanne, Carlos's wife of three weeks, who was grieving for her lost husband. Deonna and Debbie drove to a florist. Deonna purchased a flower arrangement and then drove to see her heartbroken friend. They hugged for a long while, saying nothing, only trembling with sorrow and sobbing. Some information was still not released, so Suzanne was unaware that her husband had burned in the flames of a helicopter accident. Deonna knew the details but didn't have the heart to say anything.

Deonna and the kids spent the next few days at my side in the intensive care unit. There were tubes in every orifice of my body. I don't remember waking up, but Deonna said I kept motioning for something to write on. I couldn't talk with all the life support tubes but finally was able to write a simple word: "Carlos?" I wrote it and then tapped the pencil on the notepad demanding an answer. I did this several times.

Deonna didn't want to be the one to tell me that Carlos was dead, so she quickly sent for Dr. Franklin, who was in a nearby room. Doc Franklin, meaning well, told me that Carlos died on impact.

I knew better and quickly became agitated and was crying and shaking my head, "No! No!" I seldom shed tears, but when I learned for certain that Carlos had not survived, I couldn't hold them back.

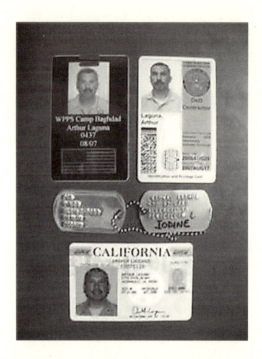

Insurgents posted Art's IDs on the internet

All 5 Blackwater Americans KIA on 1/23/2007 leaving Iraq, going home

You Have To Live Hard To Be Hard

U.S. Ambassador Zalmay Khalilzad speaks at the memorial

Ambassador Richard Griffin speaking at Art's Funeral Services in Sacramento, Calif.

Art's Funeral Detail

Patriot Riders line the entrance to Art's Funeral Services

Dan and Art Laguna while Art was active duty in Baghdad 2005

Art was teased about his shirt on Aloha Friday's (Hawaiian Shirt Day)

Art received an award for heroism in Calif. for flying one of his life saving missions

Blackwater Air Memorial Picture. The 5 guys killed in action on 23 January 2007

Welcome Home from friends and neighbors. Flags lined the street for a mile.

Flag pole and memorial place by our friends and neighbors in backyard.

Flag pole placed in back yard from friends and neighbors

Memorial Stone from our friends and neighbors

Dan and Sec. of State Condoleezza Rice February 2007. Sec. Rice expressing her condolences

Dan and President Bush on one of his surprise visits to Baghdad June 2006

Dan and U.S. Ambassador Zalmay Khalizad 28 May 2006 on LZ Washington, Baghdad

Polish Ambassador Pietrzyk pinning on the Polish Silver Star given for his rescue in an assassination attempt on his life. First one given to an American since WWII

You Have To Live Hard To Be Hard

L to R Gen. David H.Petraeus, Dan Laguna, U.S. Ambassador Ryan C. Crocker, and Polish Ambassador Pietrzyk

Dan and Ross Perot at a Congressional Medal of Honor dinner in South Carolina 1993

Carlos Guerrero - Best friend who lost his life in our helicopter accident on 20 July 1994

Dr. Kevin James – Doctor who saved my life and leg on the night of my helicopter accident 7/20/1994

YOU HAVE TO LIVE HARD TO BE HARD

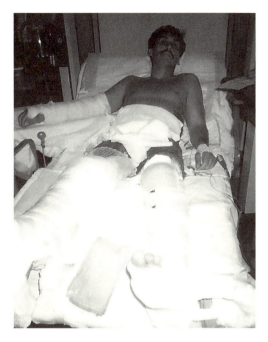

Recovering in Burn Unit in Texas – August 1994

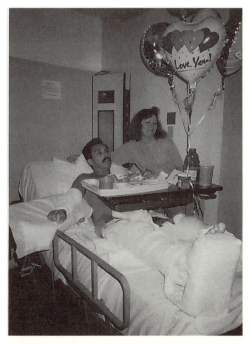

My wife, Deonna on my birthday – Burn Unit Texas 4 August 1994

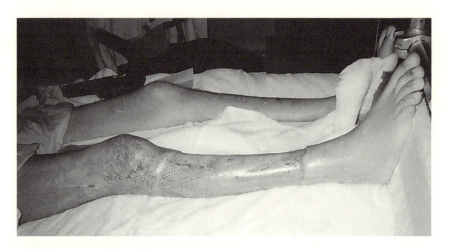

Dan's burned leg after healing from skin grafts – Hospital at Ft. Campbell, KY

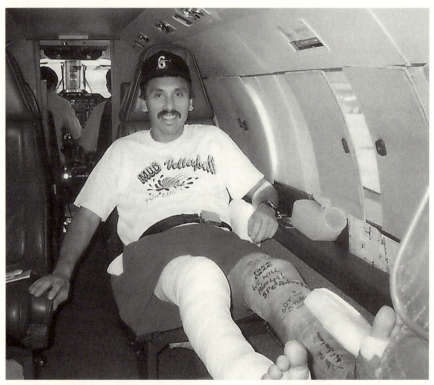

Dan leaving the Burn Center in Texas on a private jet headed to the hospital at Ft. Campbell, KY

You Have To Live Hard To Be Hard

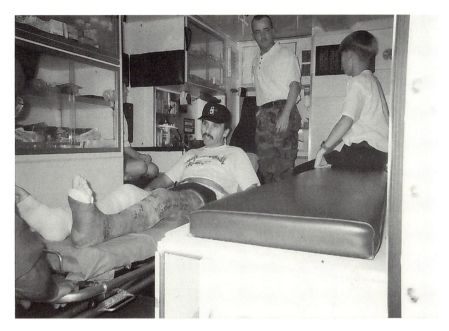

Dan riding to the Ft. Campbell Hospital in ambulance with son's Jason and Art

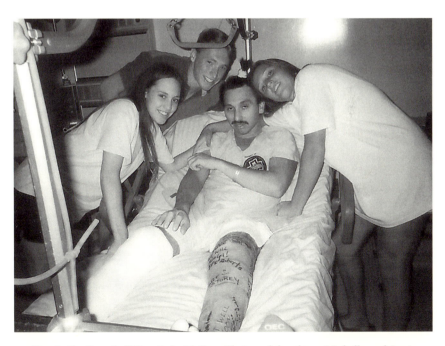

Dan in Ft. Campbell Hospital with Son, Chris and daughters Michelle and Jamie

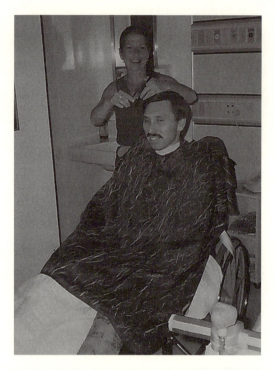

Sherry gives Dan his first haircut since his accident. Still in hospital at Ft. Campbell, KY

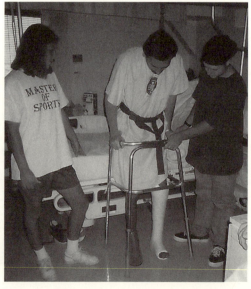

Dan taking first steps with nurse and daughter, Jamie at his side

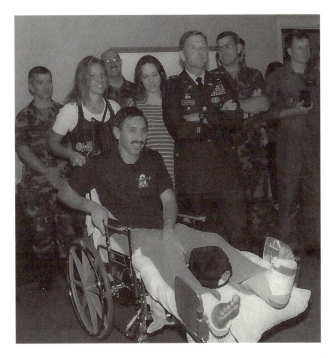

My escape from the hospital for Bob Witter's promotion. Gen. Bryan (Doug) Brown to my left, daughters, Jamie and Michelle behind me, Doc Franklin to the left side of Gen. Brown

Dan doing physical therapy with his daughter Jamie

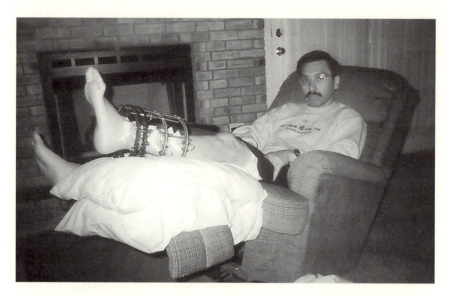

Dan recovering from surgery to lengthen the bone in his leg in order to straighten his leg

Dan hands the baton to Richard Clark on the Aloha 140 mile relay approx. 1974

YOU HAVE TO LIVE HARD TO BE HARD

Dan Laguna instructor at the Special Forces School Ft. Bragg, NC

CHAPTER ELEVEN
Burn Unit (BAMC)

As we continued to drive to the funeral luncheon, the memories of Art and Carlos and their awful deaths got the better of me. It had been a very emotional week. Deonna reached up and wiped a tear from my cheek.

As I tried to change the subject, I said, "I'm glad I went back to Baghdad early so I was there when Art died."

Deonna squeezed my hand and agreed, "I'm glad you were there, too."

I responded, "I can't imagine how bad I would feel if Art and the others had died while I was away." We drove along quietly for a minute, and then I said to her, "You know I need to go back soon."

This time it was Deonna's turn to wipe away her own tears. She said, "I know you do."

I replied, "It's my job and the guys need me."

"You don't have to explain. I know the kind of guy I married all those years ago. If you need to go back, you know I love you and I'll be here."

Deonna understood that just like all those years ago after my helicopter accident when I was so determined to fly again that I needed to go back and face my demons. It was the only way I could heal and get over that terrible day. If I would have sat at home and felt sorry for myself, dwelling on that day, I would have sunk into depression, and who knows what would have happened?

There were a few more quiet minutes. We were approaching the church and would soon be talking to family and friends again. I knew I would be facing a lot of questions from well-intentioned people. They would be asking about the day Art was shot down, and I didn't like the idea of explaining that day over and over.

The parking lot was full, and many people were making their way into the church. Cars continued to pull up to the church after we had arrived. I was surprised to see so many loved ones and friends who had taken the time to pay their respects. Hundreds of people had attended the funeral and graveside services. Art had so many friends from the various jobs he had held, and all of them wanted to honor him and his family. It was heartwarming to see so many who were moved to tears.

As I parked and opened my car door, I breathed deeply, knowing I would be talking with people I had not seen for decades. There were some old friends from high school that I hadn't spoken with since 1972. It would be good to see them, but I was apprehensive about where the conversations would go. Deonna and I walked over to my mother's car, and I opened her door and helped her out of the car. Mom's eyes were still red from the tears, and she had a Kleenex in her hand.

She wiped her nose and said, "Thank you, Danny."

As I held my mom's arm, I walked her toward the church. As we slowly walked along the sidewalk to the door, I thought about the long recovery in the burn unit after my helicopter crash.

A few days later, after I was stabilized to the point that I could breathe without a respirator, a special burn team from Brooke Army Medical Center (BAMC) in San Antonio, Texas arrived to transfer me to their burn unit. The burn unit doctors were not sure I would survive, and there was some debate about whether they could save my right leg or not. Before I could be transported I had to be stable enough to be removed from the breathing machine.

My Special Operations Unit paid for all the expenses for Deonna to accompany me there in Texas. During the long flight to San Antonio Deonna had to stay in her seat but was allowed to get up when I became agitated. She stood and held my hand and stroked my hair. I was glad she was there with me.

I hallucinated quite a bit because of the morphine. "Deonna, I keep seeing dead, burned people."

Deonna calmly said, "I know Danny, but it's not real. The morphine is making you hallucinate. Just close your eyes and try to rest."

As she stroked my hair, I was able to relax somewhat and rest. She reassured me that the things I was seeing weren't real. Although I kept seeing things, I wasn't troubled anymore, because I trusted what she was telling me. I was so grateful that she was there with me.

When we landed in San Antonio, an ambulance took me to the hospital and then took Deonna to the guesthouse to drop off her luggage before they took her to the hospital to be with me. It was around midnight.

Deonna visited me every day at the hospital and worried that one morning she would be told that I had died during the night. She knew that burn victims often lived a few weeks and died. Because I was always covered, she had never seen the burns, but even with the many layers of gauze wrapped around my right leg, it looked small because so much flesh had been burned away.

When my brother Art heard about the accident, he knew I would need blood and skin grafts, so he immediately flew to San Antonio to offer his blood and skin. We all appreciated his offer, but the doctors would not consent to using his blood because there was a very strict procedure for testing and it wasn't practical for Art to donate his skin.

At the time, the AIDS epidemic was big news. There were many reports of HIV-tainted blood being given to hospital patients during surgery. Deonna was very concerned about this, but it was her responsibility to consent to my receiving blood transfusions. Approving the transfusions, with her concerns about tainted blood, was one of the hardest things she ever did.

The same night that I arrived at the burn center in Texas, Deonna was leaving the hospital when she ran into Doc Shepherd, a friend who had previously served as the TF160 flight surgeon. He asked her what she was doing there, and she told him about my accident. He told her that he was an anesthesiologist. The two of them arranged for Doc Shepherd to become my anesthesiologist for my many upcoming surgeries. This made Deonna feel much more at ease about my upcoming surgery.

The TF160 was paying for Deonna's room at the guesthouse and for her meals, but she had no vehicle and was unable to go to the store for food. It was a one-mile walk each way to the nearest store, and it was the hottest part of the summer. Instead, she ate from vending machines for weeks. She was given certificates that allowed her to eat in the hospital cafeteria: but it was only open during visiting hours, and she didn't want to use visiting time to eat. She wanted to spend every minute with me.

One afternoon between visiting hours, Deonna sat in her hotel room watching television. She kept getting a prompting to "leave the room." She didn't recognize it as a prompting and thought these were her own thoughts. She didn't want to leave the room, because it was too hot outside and there was no place to go and nothing to do, so she continued to sit and watch TV. The thought just kept coming to her with those same three words "leave the room." After the third time, she decided that she would go downstairs to the lobby to get a little exercise.

As she stepped off the elevator, there stood a friend, Andrew Leigh, a man who had lived in Ft. Campbell, Kentucky, and was a member of our church. Many times he had visited us in our home but had recently been transferred to San Antonio to the Army Physician Assistant School. Deonna was alone, frightened for the life of her husband, and needed a friend. The good Lord provided one by sending Andrew Leigh. If Deonna had not come down to the lobby when she had, she wouldn't have known he was there, and I would not have received the blessings this good man could provide.

When they met in the lobby, each said at the same time, "What are you doing here?"

After she explained her reason for being there, Andrew arranged his schedule to include frequent visits to my bedside. He brought books and magazines, but most importantly, he gave me priesthood blessings prior to my many surgeries over the next couple of months.

On July 27th, one week after the accident, it was time for my first skin graft surgery. The doctors took skin from my left side down my torso, stomach, hip, and thigh. After the surgery, Deonna was shocked at my appearance. In order to graft the burned area they have to shave off a thin layer of skin from the donor site and put it through a machine that puts holes in it to allow it to stretch and cover a larger area from the burn site. This leaves a nasty wound.

After that thin layer of skin has been removed, they covered it with something that looked like cheesecloth or gauze. Body fluids ooze through the cloth, and over several days, it dries and becomes a nasty looking scab. After several days, the nurses had to wheel me into the room where they did the daily scrubbings. They would wet me down and pull the gauze off, leaving pink new skin. It was painful and often hurt worse than the burns. I had to be re-grafted on the back of the heel over the Achilles tendon and a couple areas of my leg. That meant I went through that procedure twice.

Visitors to burn units are required to scrub their hands with antibacterial soap, and wear gowns, gloves, booties and even masks and caps prior to going to the patient's bedside. If visitors left the room, they were required to repeat the same steps before they came in again. The room was kept at over 80 degrees or more. The doctors had heat lamps on the patients to dry up the donor sites and help them heal quicker. The overheated room was very uncomfortable for visitors, especially Deonna, who was there for hours each day.

July 28th was our daughter, Jamie's eighteenth birthday. Deonna called her to tell her happy birthday, but she was without her parents, taking care of our household, and very worried about me. Deonna assured her everything would be all right.

The next day, Dr. O'Neil, a Task Force Flight Surgeon, and Randy Jones, a guy from our unit safety board, came to interview me about the accident. The military took these accidents seriously, and they needed to know exactly how the accident had happened. It had only been two days since my surgery, and I was still in ICU and still out of it from the morphine. After the interview, Deonna asked me what I had told them but I didn't remember them being there.

I don't remember much of the first forty days, but Deonna tells me I would wake up periodically. Different family members, including my parents, were at the hospital in San Antonio, but I don't remember seeing any of them either.

I was finally transferred out of the ICU on August 1st. Not long after that, Carlos's parents came to see me. They had been waiting for me to be transferred out of the Burn ICU to the B Ward of the Burn Center before they visited me. I was still on morphine so my recollection of that day was a little vague.

I remember looking up and seeing Mrs. Guerrero walking through the door. The moment our eyes met, Mrs. Guerrero started crying. I could see the anguish on her face, and it was more painful to me than the burns. With Carlos's parents standing there in front of me, it became an instant reminder of something I wished I could forget. Mrs. Guerrero asked me in half English and half Spanish if her Carlos suffered. I had to lie to save her any further pain. I could not bear telling her that he burned to death.

I said, "No, Mrs. Guerrero. Carlos died on impact."

She asked, "Are you sure?"

I replied, "Yes, ma'am". As she wept, I continued, "If I could I would change places right now with Carlos. I would burn the rest of my body if it would bring him back."

Deonna was with them, and I remember Mr. Guerrero hugging her as they both cried.

Carlos's mother then looked toward me, wiping her tears, and said, "I know you tried to save Carlos. Thank you for trying to save my Carlos."

I felt so undeserving. I wished a thousand times I could change places with Carlos. He was younger than I was, only thirty-two, with two kids, one only a baby. Carlos had remarried just twenty days prior to the accident. His life was on a new course for success. He would always tell me how happy he was again and how much he loved Suzanne. My physical pain was temporary and tolerable, but the emotional pain was unbearable. Why did I live and not Carlos? I have asked myself that question many times.

I eventually came to the conclusion that only God knew the answer to that question and that I needed to have the faith and strength to do whatever it was the Lord left me here to do. I survived miraculously for a reason, and I've spent my time trying to know that reason, vowing to be the best person I can be and to help others.

Early one morning, a twelve-year-old boy was assigned to a bed next to me in my room. I was barely conscious because of the morphine but heard the nurses calling to him. The boy had bad burns, and the nurses needed to move him to the shower for the terribly painful but necessary scrubbing of his burns.

The boy's last name was Guerrero, the same last name as my best friend Carlos.

The nurses kept calling him, "Mr. Guerrero . . . Mr. Guerrero

... we need to move you to the showers for scrubbing . . . Mr. Guerrero!"

As soon as I heard them calling Mr. Guerrero, my heart began pounding and I tried to sit up. I thought Carlos had somehow survived and that they had put him in my room. The nurses saw me struggling and realized that they were calling the same name of my lost friend. They came quickly and explained about the boy, apologizing for upsetting me. Still confused, I fell back in my bed, crying out for Carlos.

Being in the bed next to this little boy, I learned that his parents were struggling financially and didn't have the money to stay in a hotel because they were from out of town. Later that day when Deonna came to visit, I told her about it, and we agreed that she would give them some money to help them stay while their son was in the burn unit. They didn't speak English; but somehow Deonna made them understand why she was giving them money and they thanked her.

The doctors wanted me to eat more, because I was only eating a few bites at every meal. I was very thirsty, however, and because the doctors could not get me to eat enough, they gave me a high-calorie drink that was very sweet. I needed the nutrients and calories in that drink but I didn't like it and kept asking for plain water.

When the doctors and nurses were out of the room, Deonna would rush to get me a full glass of ice-cold water and say, "Danny, they're not looking. Quick! Drink!"

On August 4th, two weeks after the accident, I have a vague memory of Deonna at the foot of my bed with several balloons.

She stood there smiling and said, "Happy Birthday, Danny. I love you."

Susan Davis, the wife of a former B Company Commander, was there as well. Deonna was taking pictures but the hospital staff came in and told her it wasn't allowed.

Deonna objected, "But it's his birthday!"

They insisted that she couldn't take pictures, because it could cause an explosion, so she reluctantly stopped.

Deonna told me that a few days later I seemed more coherent and had a conversation with her and wanted to know how she was told about the accident and what she and the kids experienced on the night of the accident. Although I don't remember much about that day, she said I was very emotional and broke down crying after I talked about Carlos.

As we spoke, I realized the kids had been home alone for a couple of weeks. School was about to start and the kids needed to be enrolled and get school clothes and supplies. Deonna didn't want to hear it, but I told her that she needed to leave me and go home to care for the kids. Reluctantly, she made arrangements to go home.

Shortly after her return home I called her. She could tell by my voice that I was crying. The pain was unbearable. She began to feel guilty about leaving me alone in such a bad condition. Deonna called Dr. Franklin and asked if he could arrange for our son Chris, who was in the Task Force at the time, to spend some time at the burn center with me.

Dr. Franklin convinced the Task force Commander, Colonel Brown, to allow Chris the time away, so one day he showed up at my bedside. His support helped keep my spirits up during those painful days.

Both my legs were broken and I was not able to get out of bed and walk around like all the other burn patients. There was a pecking order there in B Ward it seemed, and the way it worked was that the one who had been there the longest got the bed by the window. It took a while but I eventually got the bed by the window. I really liked to be by the window, because I was not able to get out of bed and walk around yet and because I could at least look out and enjoy the view.

One day while I was daydreaming and looking out the window, I saw lights flashing in the distance. I kept watching and soon I could see a fire engine with flashing lights coming down the road toward the hospital. I thought; *I sure hope no one gets burned.* I kept watching, and the fire engine kept getting closer and closer until it stopped in front of the hospital.

A moment later a fire alarm sounded and the fire warning lights in the hospital started flashing. Just then all the other burn patients started walking out and a nurse came and shut the door to my room. I was convinced the hospital was on fire. I was the only patient left in the room and could not get out of bed on my own. In desperation, I started pressing the call button but no one answered. I yelled for help, but no one came.

I thought because of all the commotion going on, the hospital staff had forgotten to evacuate me with the other patients, so with my mind racing, I began looking at my options. Nobody else was there, so I had to save myself. I tried to maneuver myself closer to the window by grabbing the curtain and pulling my bed closer. My intention was to break the window with whatever I could get my hands on and pull myself out through the window. I absolutely refused to burn again, and I couldn't walk to safety, so my only option was to throw myself out of the fourth floor window. At that moment, it seemed better than burning again.

About then, patients began to return to their rooms. One of the nurses walked in and realized what I was trying to do.

She ran to my bedside and said, "I'm so sorry, Mr. Laguna. I should have told you. I'm so sorry. It was just a fire drill."

A little embarrassed, I relaxed back into my bed, and stared out the window.

Many times in the middle of the night I would wake from a bad dream, reliving the night of the accident. I dreamed I was on fire and could not extinguish it, and Carlos calling for me over and over. It got to the point I didn't want to close my eyes, because I was afraid to fall asleep. I tried to avoid it, but sometimes I called out loud in my sleep. That was when some of my night nurses would come over and ask if I wanted to talk.

The pain was severe, even with the morphine. But in an indescribable way, I felt I deserved the pain. The sound of Carlos's voice, screaming for help, and my inability to help him never left my mind. I was always conscious of the fact that my best friend had burned to death right in front of me, and I hadn't been able to do anything about it. The level of guilt cannot be expressed in words.

I began to want the pain as a kind of atonement for not saving Carlos. Suffering my own pain was the least I could do for him. My best friend had died, and I had lived. That very thought was painful. It was my time to suffer. In a strange way, I felt like I owed some suffering to him.

I had spent weeks on morphine and when I became sensible enough to realize this, I demanded that no morphine be administered to me ever again.

The nurse objected. "What do you mean no more morphine?"

"That's exactly what I mean. No more morphine."

She went to get the doctor, who tried to explain how necessary it was. "Mr. Laguna, we need to scrub your burns every day. There's no way you can endure the pain without the morphine."

I insisted they give me none and refused to let them attempt it. There were a number of conflicts over the use of morphine in the following months. As the morphine wore off, the pain became very intense and I felt I was paying the necessary price for not saving Carlos. Even later skin grafts were done without morphine following the surgery.

The skin grafts were troublesome, and in some areas they had to be re-grafted. The surgery involved taking more healthy skin and re-grafting some of the deeper burns on my leg, including my Achilles tendon.

Our son Chris was there when I came out of the operating room. I had instructed him before I had gone into surgery that he was to wake me up if they hooked me up to morphine. Well, Chris was an obedient son, and he knew I was serious about that, so he woke me up when the nurses brought me back to my room.

I heard Chris say, "Hey, Dad, wake up. You're hooked up to morphine."

Still dazed from the anesthesia and morphine, I could hear and understand what he was saying, so I clumsily reached for the morphine line and began pulling it out.

The nurse came in and tried to stop me, saying, "You only need it for a while. We'll disconnect it later."

Afraid of becoming addicted and feeling like I still owed Carlos, I refused and kept struggling with the nurse. She finally disconnected the morphine drip.

Several weeks after my accident, my leg in its original cast, the orthopedic surgeon decided that my left leg bones were healing crooked and had to be reset. There were five breaks that had not fully healed, and each of them needed to be reset.

The nurse came in to explain the situation and said, "Mr. Laguna, I know how you feel about the morphine, but we'll need to give you some for this procedure."

I said to the nurse, "We already had this discussion."

She wheeled me down to the orthopedic room and the doctor said, "Go ahead and give him the morphine now."

The nurse looked at me, and I gave her a firm glare.

She stated, "He won't take the morphine, Doctor."

The doctor looked at me like I was from another planet. "What do you mean you won't take morphine?"

After a few minutes of trying to reason with me, they finally gave up trying. I deserved the pain. They couldn't give me enough pain. It was my duty to suffer like Carlos had. I rolled up a small towel and stuffed it in my mouth.

The doctor said, "Here we go."

I muffled through the towel, "Okay."

The doctor began yanking and twisting my leg. As he reset all five fractures, I tried not to scream but couldn't help groaning and grunting through the towel. I began to sweat profusely, and the doctor stopped for a moment.

"Now do you want the shots?"

I shook my head, indicating "no morphine, keep going."

As soon as his gruesome work was done, he said, "We have it. Go ahead and cast it."

About that time, the pain got the better of me. I passed out. Later, I awoke in my room and I had a new cast on my leg.

During all the weeks I spent in the burn recovery ward, I kept hearing nurses and some of the other patients whispering and talking about me. They saw that my hair was much too long for army standards and wondered who I really was. I had a lot of visitors who were of high rank and they noticed I was getting a lot of special attention. I could hear them in the hallway debating with each other and saying that I was a special agent and that I was probably shot down in South America. A few times they would address me directly and ask me what had happened.

During the two months in the burn center, I had received some special guests. General Brown, the former Task Force Commander, Major Rhonda Cornum, MD, a former POW during the first Gulf War, and other guests in civilian clothes stopped by to see me. General Cody and his entire family flew to San Antonio to be at my bedside. I received phone calls from all over the world. This started some rumors among the hospital staff and even some of the other patients.

They continually asked me, "Why are these high-ranking guys always coming to see you? Who are you?"

Of course, all I could say was, "I'm just a regular army guy who was injured in a helicopter accident."

None of them believed me and typically commented something like, "You must be a Special Agent. I'll bet you were shot down in a black ops mission or something."

These rumors persisted the whole time I was in the burn center, and all the while I had to keep up my "regular army guy" story.

After a few weeks, Chris had to go back to Ft. Campbell, and I was on my own again. Being alone again, enduring severe pain twenty-four hours a day and constantly in my sleep hearing Carlos screaming for my help, I began to get depressed.

Time passed so slowly. It felt as if a week were a year. I asked to be transferred to the hospital at Ft. Campbell to be near family and friends, but they would not let me leave the burn unit until my grafts had healed properly.

After a few weeks of depression, I finally received the news I was waiting for. Deonna called and told me that Doc Miller, my unit doctor, was flying in to pick me up in a private chartered jet to take me to the hospital at Ft. Campbell.

As the hospital was preparing me to leave in a day or two, a General in charge of the hospital came in to see me.

He stood by my bed with a puzzled look and said, "Who are you?"

I replied, "What do you mean, Sir?"

He said, "I have worked at this hospital a long time and we have never had a patient of ours go anywhere by private jet. Our patients always travel on military flights."

I smiled and said, "Sir I belong to a military unit with very special people in it and they go out of their way to take care of us."

He queried, "You are in the army?"

"Yes, Sir."

Then he said, "You're an army pilot."

"Yes, Sir."

He thought about that for a few seconds then said, "So let me see. They are picking up an army pilot in a private jet with his own doctor on board."

I smiled and said, "Yes, Sir."

With a mystified look on his face, he said, "Right. Have a good flight." He turned and walked away with that mystified look on his face.

A couple of days before I was transferred, my doctor noticed a dime-size spot that was not healing. They decided to keep me a few extra days, delaying my return home. That huge disappointment had me depressed again, and I kind of gave up. I felt I was never going to go home.

Early one morning a few days later, I was lying in bed and heard a lot of commotion out in the hallway. I could hear the sound of people running, and thought there was some kind of emergency with one of the patients. Everyone began sitting up in bed and wondering what all the commotion was about.

Suddenly, two men burst into my room shouting, "Dan Laguna, we are Navy SEALS here to break you out. The jet is on the ramp with engines running and ready to go."

I looked up in surprise and realized it was just Doc Miller and Doc Shepherd from my Special Operations Unit having a little fun and trying to cheer me up. It worked.

They threw some clothes to the nurse and said, "Get him ready to fly. We don't have much time."

This little stunt by my friends just confirmed all the rumors and suspicions that I was not just a regular army guy.

A few of the nurses and patients made comments as I was being rolled out the door, "We knew you weren't just a regular army guy."

They quickly loaded me on a gurney and rolled me down the hall to the elevator.

As we passed the nurse's station, Doc Miller continued the ruse. "Hurry up with those medical records. We don't have much time!"

They whisked me down to the waiting ambulance; loaded me in, and then Doc Miller jumped in the back with me and hollered, "Let's go!"

As the ambulance drove away, we laughed together, and I felt better than I had felt for a long time.

Doc Shepherd, laughing about how well their plan worked said, "Dan, what did you think of all that?"

I chuckled, "Now I know no one will believe my story about being a regular army guy."

As we laughed, the pain subsided. The drive to the airport took about twenty minutes.

Doc Miller explained, "The airplane is not set up to carry a patient lying down, so you might get a little uncomfortable."

I told him, "I'll do whatever it takes. I'm just thankful to be going home."

When we arrived at the airport the ambulance backed right up to the airplane. They had a difficult time loading me because my legs were not able to bend. When they were finally able to get me inside they put me on a rear-facing seat with my legs extended and resting on another seat. It definitely wasn't the most comfortable way to fly, but I was determined not to complain after what everyone had gone through to make this happen.

Despite the high level of confidentiality and the news blackout about the crash, newspapers had been getting little snippets of information about the accident and my condition. To avoid any news reporters, I was flown to Outlaw Airfield, a small civilian airport near Ft. Campbell. Deonna and all our kids, as well as Doc Franklin, some friends, a couple of Colonels from the unit, and Sherry Brynick, my Company Commander's wife, were all there.

Some of the people who had not seen me since before the accident were surprised to see me so frail. Prior to the accident, I weighed around two hundred pounds, but now was down to one hundred forty-five pounds. I was weak and pale, and I had a long road to recovery ahead of me.

CHAPTER TWELVE
Recovery at BACH

MEANWHILE, WE ARRIVED AT THE church luncheon that was being held by members of our church after the funeral. I opened the church door for my mother and wife. We walked into the foyer and were met by hundreds of people I hadn't seen for many years. I was especially happy to see my friend Curtis Lien, who was my best friend since first grade all the way through high school, there with his wife, Lisa, and son, Neil. I also saw another good friend from church, Mark LaForte. His family was instrumental in converting my family to the LDS religion. Mom was overwhelmed by the outpouring of love everyone had for our family.

She turned and said, "He must have touched thousands of lives."

I replied, "More than we will ever know."

There were people from all over the country there to show respect for Art and our family. I saw many familiar faces; however, several stood out and I wanted to introduce them to my mother and Deonna.

I escorted both of them to meet someone from the State Department and said, "Mom, I'd like you to meet Ambassador Griffin; he is over the World Wide Personal Protection Service (WPPS) program from the State Department overseeing the Baghdad program."

The ambassador reached to shake Mom's hand, holding it warmly as he said, "Mrs. Laguna, I'm so sorry about the loss of your son. He was a great man doing great work."

Mom thanked him politely, and then Deonna and I stood and spoke with the ambassador for a few minutes. As we spoke I noticed dozens of old friends milling about and talking with one another. There was the President of Presidential Airways, talking with Danny Carroll. Danny was a very close friend who we nicknamed "Rudy" after the character in the movie *Rudy*. Danny (Rudy) Carroll was the Program Manager for all Blackwater ground teams in Baghdad. In another area were a few of the door gunners who had worked with Art. I introduced each of them to Deonna and my mom.

There was a group of Folsom Prison guards talking with a group of deputies from the Sheriff Department. Others were from the California National Guard unit where Art had served.

I saw several of my old high school friends, many old neighbors and hundreds of members of our church, all there to pay their respects. My mind was drawn back to the days when many of these people didn't believe my brothers and I would ever amount to anything.

We walked into the large gymnasium where the luncheon was being served. Deonna brought a plate of food, but I didn't feel much like eating and refused it.

Mom sat across the table from me and said, "I'm so glad you were there when Art died. It gives me comfort knowing you were there."

She had repeated that same thing over and over.

Some of Mom's friends were sitting near her and they carried on a conversation in Spanish. Although I didn't speak the language well, I had grown up hearing it, so I could understand much of what they were saying. One of the ladies told my mom that Art and I were heroes.

She said, "Our community needed a hero, someone for the kids to look up to."

Another said, "Just look what your sons have accomplished! Our people are minorities, and your sons gave us someone to be proud of."

I suppose these words were true, and they certainly uplifted my mother. We were dirt poor as kids growing up. We had worn-out clothes and picked tomatoes with immigrant workers. We ate from our own gardens and lived on the poor side of town, well below the poverty level. We were disrespected minority kids just like so many others from our side of town. Art came from nothing yet had accomplished so much in life. Now people were here from all over the country to honor him. It was good for Mom to see how much these people loved and respected Art.

People at the church luncheon would frequently come to me and speak highly of my military service, but it always made me feel uncomfortable. I always redirected their compliments to Art.

Danny Carroll asked me, "Why was Art always smiling so much?"

I responded, "Art was one of the best helicopter pilots in all of the military. He once told me in Baghdad that he felt like he made it to the Super Bowl of flying when he came to work for me. He just loved what he did."

It was true. Art smiled from sunup to sundown and everyone loved to be around him.

The ambassador said, "I know that diplomats often made special requests for Art to escort them around."

We spent a couple of hours at the church before the guests began to go home. The many kind words from so many people had been uplifting to all of us. My mood was improving, and Deonna could see it.

She reached for my hand and said, "Art's girls want to talk with you."

She motioned to Tammy, Sherri, and Erin. These were Art's grown daughters, and they had wanted some private time with me but didn't want to interrupt me. As soon as I heard it, I quickly went over to see them.

"Hey, you didn't need to wait for me. I am always happy to give you some private time."

We walked to an empty hallway where Tammy said, "Uncle Danny, tell us more about Dad and what happened."

These beautiful girls were heartbroken at the loss of their father and needed some kind of closure. I told them the whole story and reminded them how much their dad loved them.

They were glad to hear the whole story and wiped away tears.

I continued, "Your dad always spoke about you. He told me a thousand times how much he loved each of you."

The words were comforting and they thanked me.

After I hugged each of them, I said, "You can be very proud of your dad, his life, and even his death."

The girls were happy to have had a more personal understanding of their father's death.

I went back to the luncheon table and Mom said, "Is everyone ready to go to the American Legion Hall?"

Our family had been invited to use the American Legion Hall in Rio Linda for a smaller gathering of friends and family. After they had heard about Art's death, the Legionnaires contacted Mom and invited her to use the hall at no cost. It was a kind gesture, so Mom accepted the invitation.

As things wound down at the luncheon and people began to leave, my mind would drift and I would think of that most happy day when I was able to transfer from the hospital in San Antonio to the hospital near my family on Ft. Campbell. As we drove away from Outlaw Field, my kids were allowed to ride to the hospital in the back of the ambulance with me, and Deonna rode in front with the driver. Compared with how discouraged I had felt while alone in San Antonio, this short ride to the hospital put me on top of the world. I was determined to withstand the pain and work hard on my recovery.

The doctors were surprised that I had survived, and nobody believed I could avoid the amputation of my burned leg. The general opinion of my condition was that I would be lucky to ever walk again. Running, flying, even staying in the army was not even considered a possibility. Although I didn't say much to anyone, my plans for the future were to get right back to my old job. Walking wasn't my goal. Neither was running. I wanted to be able to walk, run, fly, and re-qualify as a Special Operations operator in my unit, and failure was not an option.

After I was settled in my room on the fourth floor of Blanchfield

Army Community Hospital, with my smiling wife and children surrounding my bed, I thought, *I'm going to like this hospital.*

As we visited on that first afternoon, Deonna, Steve and Debbie Bowyer, and our kids heard me talk about the night of the accident. It was the first time any of them had heard me talk about what happened. After I told them about being miraculously removed from the helicopter, Deonna had to sit down and gather her wits. She wasn't expecting to hear such a story. The nurses needed to get me settled so Deonna walked out with Debbie Bowyer as she and Steve left to go home.

Deonna returned a few minutes later and exclaimed, "If I would have known that you were miraculously saved, I wouldn't have spent so much time worrying that I would lose you!"

I was surprised at her response, because she actually sounded angry with me.

She continued her chastisement, "I thought you might die and was worried sick all this time. You should have told me earlier about how you were saved. I wouldn't have worried so much. God wouldn't save you like that just to let you die later."

I didn't know whether to laugh or cry at her reaction, but said, "I'm sorry. I guess I should have told you sooner."

The first night in Blanchfield, the nurses came in and said it was time to get me ready for bed.

They had a puzzled look on their faces and one of them said, "We have never had a patient with serious burns before, and we don't have the necessary medical supplies to dress your wounds. Can you help us make a list of the things we will need?"

Of course I was more than willing to help them out. After two months at the burn center, watching the burn nurse every day, I knew the drill. I gave them a list of supplies they would need, and the few items they didn't have were sent via FedEx.

I was extremely anxious to start some kind of workout routine again and get back into shape. I worked out daily in our TF160th gym with weights before my accident and so I thought I would get a set of dumbbell weights and start working out in my hospital bed. I asked one of my nurses if she could get me a set of forty-pound dumbbell weights for me to use in bed. She looked at me kind of funny and acted a little reluctant but agreed to find some weights for me. It wasn't long and she came into my room with the forty-pound weights. With a look of concern on her face she handed them to me, and the realization of how weak I was hit me like a ton of bricks. I could not even lift one of them. I was so embarrassed. I had to ask her to get me a set of ten-pound weights instead. She left and came back a short time later with a set of ten-pound dumbbell weights. They felt like forty pounds to me. How could this be? At that moment I realized my frail state and knew I needed to do something about it. I worked out with those weights every day several times a day to regain my strength.

Every day was a challenge for the new staff to care for me. My first shower at Blanchfield was comical. They did not have a bed like the special bed at the burn ward, so they improvised. They took all the bedding and mattress off one of the gurneys and put me on it and then pushed me into a room that had a regular shower. It was obvious that the gurney was not going to fit into the shower so they pushed me up against the wall and hosed me down right there. By the time we were done the floor was flooded all the way down the hall to the nurse's station.

After about one week of the nurses giving me bed showers, I thought Deonna needed to be involved with one of these memorable moments. Deonna had not yet seen my burned leg and I wanted her to see it. I guess it was a test to see if she would still love me. It looked pretty bad. She was scared but I asked her to look anyway. She got a little weak in the knees but got over it quickly. Now she says it looks beautiful to her. She really must love me.

Over time, the showers became less messy. I really never had any complaints with the medical staff at the Fort Campbell hospital; they always went out of their way to care for me. In my opinion, you have to have a heart of gold to become a nurse. I certainly felt that way about all my nurses.

One day a doctor who was treating another burn patient came to see me with his nurse.

The doctor asked, "Would you be willing to come and visit one of our patients?"

I said, "Yes sir. Why?"

The nurse replied, "He's been a difficult patient. He has second-degree burns on his arms and face, nowhere near as bad as your burns, but he keeps asking for painkillers."

The doctor thought the patient needed to toughen up a little bit. They thought that if I spent some time with him, he would get a better perspective on his condition.

My nurse helped me into a wheelchair and covered me with a sheet, and then pushed me into the other burn patient's room. She introduced us and then left the room. I asked him how he was burned, and he said he was camping with his family. Their campfire wouldn't stay lit, so he threw some gasoline on the fire. It erupted violently, burning his arms and face.

He then asked me why I was in the hospital. I told him a little bit

You Have To Live Hard To Be Hard

about my accident and that I had already been in the hospital a few months. I then told him that painkillers were not always the answer; that sometimes you just had to deal with the pain.

At first my words upset him, and he asked how bad my burns were. He could not see my burns because the nurse had covered me with a sheet in the wheelchair. It wasn't my intent to see who had the worst burns. It was to try to help him realize sometimes we just needed to focus on other things and not the pain we felt.

When I pulled the sheet off my leg it was as if he just seen a ghost. We talked a little while longer about our burns. I told him I would not accept morphine and believed a person could control his or her response to pain without being dependent on drugs that were addictive.

The next day his doctor stopped by to thank me and said, "Whatever you said to him worked, because he doesn't bother the nurses for pain medication anymore."

Dr. Kevin James the orthopedic surgeon who took care of me the night of my accident came by to see me. Doc James came to my room just after visiting hours were over and said that he wanted to talk to me. Deonna had barely walked out the door, and was going home. I immediately thought he was there to tell me they were going to have to amputate my leg. I had been told that saving my burned leg was unlikely and that I should not to be surprised if they had to amputate. So that was always in the back of my mind.

I said, "Sure, Doc, what's on your mind?"

Without saying a word, he walked over and closed the door. I immediately thought, *This isn't good.*

He said that the accident investigation board had stopped by to see him and asked him some questions.

They asked, "Dr. James, in your professional opinion as head of orthopedics for this hospital, and with all the injuries that Mr. Laguna had that night, how was he able to get out of the helicopter by himself?"

He said, "There was no physical way possible for Mr. Laguna to get himself out without some kind of help."

Dr. James asked them, "What did Mr. Laguna tell you about that night?"

The head investigator said, "Mr. Laguna's story of that night, after they crashed and rolled, was that the helicopter was on fire and the engine was running. Then all of a sudden it was quiet, and he heard a voice say, "Undo your seatbelt, and you will be free."

There was a pause. The investigation board didn't believe the story was plausible, because I was still on morphine at the time I told the board what had happened. They presumed I was hallucinating.

The investigator continued, "Mr. Laguna then said the next thing he knew he was lying outside the helicopter."

Dr. James responded, "I don't know precisely what happened, but you'd better believe him. I was the attending physician that night, and I am here to tell you that with the injuries he sustained he is lucky to be alive, let alone get himself out of the helicopter."

Dr. James took a step closer to me, looking seriously into my eyes, and paused for a moment. Then he asked me, "Dan, how did you get out of the helicopter?"

I tried to give him the quick answer and avoid telling the miraculous parts, because I didn't think he would believe me. Dr. James realized I was avoiding some of the story and quickly raised his right hand gesturing for me to stop.

He said, "No, I want to hear the whole story."

So I took time to tell him the full story with all the details.

Dr. James listened intently, then said, "I knew it!" He spun around, and clapped his hands, and then turned back to me. He looked intently at me, calm, and with a slight smile, he said, "My father was a minister. I don't know if you are a religious man, but if you aren't, you'd better get that way. I want you to know that you are still alive for a reason, and you'd better figure out why that is because you couldn't have survived without God's help."

He then told me his own story about that night. He said he was at home relaxing when he received the call about a serious helicopter accident. He was told that there had been a very bad helicopter crash and that one of the pilots had some life-threatening burns and fractures. The doctors on duty that night were young, and from the tone in their voice, Dr. James knew it had to be pretty serious. They asked Dr. James to please come in to help. He rushed to the emergency room and evaluated me and then told the nurses to prepare me for emergency surgery.

Dr. James then explained that he walked out of the emergency room and straight to his office, closing the door behind him. He was troubled about how to treat my injuries and didn't expect me to survive the night. He wanted divine help. As he knelt down by his desk, he prayed for help asking God to guide his hands to do whatever was necessary to save my life and my leg.

Minutes later, in emergency surgery, he was inspired to cut the burned leg on both sides deep enough to reach good flesh. In his mind this would allow my leg to swell without cutting off circulation to the leg. He explained that this was not a normal procedure, but he felt it was an answer to his prayer. He put a metal plate in my burned right leg to hold the ankle together and then set the other leg the best he could and put a cast on it.

When I arrived at the burn center in San Antonio, the head of the burn unit, Dr. Barrillo, took one look at my leg and went to call Dr. James. He was surprised and angry and demanded to know what in the heck he was trying to do.

Dr. James tried to defend his procedure, but Dr. Barrillo insisted that if I had been sent straight to Brooke Army Medical Center after my helicopter crash, he would have immediately amputated my right leg. Dr. James was chastised, but convinced Dr. Barrillo that because he had gone that far with trying to save my leg, it wouldn't hurt to try a skin graft on it anyway.

Dr. Barrillo reluctantly agreed. Needless to say, I still have my leg. It isn't pretty, but it works well enough thanks to Dr. James and his desire to ask for divine intervention and Dr. Barrillo, who was willing to try something he didn't believe would work. Without the prayers and faith of many people, my outcome would have been significantly worse.

I've thought a lot about Dr. James over the years. There is something to say about a man who recognizes he needs that special help and has the humility to kneel down and ask God for it. After I heard his story, I gained a lot of admiration for him. One day, he pointed out that if I had been successful in my attempt to drag myself all the way back to Carlos, I would have likely been killed in the final explosion.

Even after I was discharged from the hospital, I often stopped to visit the man who saved my life and my leg. Dr. Kevin James is a man of high moral integrity, and he is now retired from the U. S. Army, operating a private practice in Charlotte, North Carolina.

Occasionally, I would ask the doctors how long it would be before I could start working out in the physical therapy room.

Their response was always the same, "You have too many badly burned tendons, ligaments and muscles. You'll probably never be able to use your leg."

I spent weeks lying in bed contemplating my bleak prognosis. One day, I realized I could just barely move my big toe. I got the idea that if I could move my toe, then maybe I could work on my foot movement in order to walk again. I started my own physical therapy program, stretching a surgical hose around my toes and trying to force my toe back and forth against the pull of the hose. At first I could barely move the toe at all, but I kept at it until weeks later I surprised the doctors by moving my foot front to back.

By then, both my broken legs were healing, and my burns were doing well, so it was time to start physical therapy. My left leg had a cast to the knee for months, and the right leg was basically one big scab. The legs had stayed in the same position for three months and neither of them could bend.

Obviously, I needed to bend my legs if I was to ever walk again. With a cast only up to my left knee now, Deonna and my daughters, Michelle and Jamie, took turns doing physical therapy on my legs. They would push and try to bend my legs at the knees and up to my chest. At first, I could barely get a bend in them. Slowly with constant exercising and help from my wife and daughters and their daily routines, I was able to bend my knees somewhat.

The next step was to put my legs over the side of the bed. I turned sideways in bed so I could get my legs to hang over the edge of the bed. Hanging my legs over the bed caused the skin on both legs to turn bright purple and clear fluids to ooze through the skin of both legs. Deonna would get a wet cloth and gently tap on my legs to get the clear fluids off. We couldn't just let it stay, because then it would dry up and become a nasty scab.

I had not put my legs over the side of the bed in three months. Each time I lowered my legs, the increased blood pressure caused immense pain, so I could only stand it for a few seconds at a time and then I would swing my legs up onto the bed again.

I did this many times during the day to try to get my legs accustomed to the blood flow again. After about a week of hanging me legs over the edge of the bed, I could bear the pain long enough to stand next to the bed with the help of a walker, and a strong person alongside me. Slowly I began to take steps, at first only one step and then back to bed I went. It drained me completely, but I did that several times a day until I could finally make it from the bed to the door which was only about six feet away. Walking six feet was much more than the doctors thought I would ever do.

It was a huge, exciting day when I was able to scuttle to the bathroom on my own. I had been using bedpans for several months. On my first solo toilet trip, while I was sitting there excited that I made it on my own, I pulled the nurse's call cord.

A nurse quickly replied over the intercom, "Mr. Laguna, is there a problem? Do you need help?"

With a big grin on my face, I explained, "I just used the toilet. This is a Kodak moment."

Over the intercom from the nurses station, I could hear applauding and laughter.

I thought to myself, *I just received a standing ovation!*

CHAPTER THIRTEEN
Physical Therapy

Dr. James, surprised at my rapid progress, came in one day and saw me walking short distances with the aid of a walker.

He told me, "As soon as you can walk the hall, circling the entire fourth floor, you can start going to the physical therapy room."

I called the physical therapy room the gym. The thought of going to the gym excited me and I began to work even harder. But that caused a temporary setback. I worked so hard that I got stress fractures in my weakened legs from being on my feet too much. I was ordered back to bed for two full weeks. The bedpan and I became friends again.

After that short recovery the doctors allowed me to begin making daily trips to the physical therapy room with a walker and a safety strap around me held by one of the physical therapist assistants. That was a big motivation for me because I felt that my recovery was finally in my own hands. The elevator was about fifty feet down the hall and that was a huge distance, almost intimidating; however, I made it all the way there and rested in the elevator. The physical therapy room was another twenty feet after I got off the elevator.

The physical therapist was a woman who told me, "Some patients feel that I am too demanding and hard on them."

I replied, "You won't have that problem with me."

She allowed me to take a few baby steps in the parallel bars and then said, "That's enough for today. You can do five more minutes tomorrow."

That tiny workout wasn't enough for me. I gave her a determined look and said, "I don't want to cause you any trouble, but I'm not leaving. I came here to work out and get in shape. Five minutes won't do."

Of course the therapist objected, "It is the doctor's orders, only five minutes."

She wasn't accustomed to rebellious patients but there was no way I would go back to bed after a five-minute workout.

I stood my ground with her. "Look, I understand your position but I am not going back to my room yet."

The therapist was upset and went to see Doc James, the orthopedic surgeon who had saved my life and my leg the night of the accident. By then Doc James recognized my determination and did not stop my daily workouts. He told the therapist to let me do whatever I wanted to do.

I began on the exercise bicycle. Riding the bike forced my knees to bend more than when I was walking so the grafted tissue behind my knee started splitting again. Blood would drip down my leg and get all over the floor, but I knew this was necessary if I wanted to walk again. After a while I quit using the walker and began using crutches.

I spent every day in that room, exercising from morning until dinner, not even stopping for lunch. After a month in the physical therapy room I asked Doc James when he would release me to finish my recovery at home.

He asked, "Do you have stairs in your house?"

I answered, "Yes, sir."

"Then you can't go home until you can walk up and down a flight of stairs."

That day when the physical therapist's assistant came to help me back to my room he walked me to the elevator like he always did, but I turned and went the opposite direction toward the stairs.

He stopped and asked, "What are you doing?"

I said, "No more elevators. I can't go home until I can walk up and down stairs."

He was not too happy, because it was time for him to go home and he knew it would take a long time to get back to my fourth floor room by using the stairs. At first it took me nearly an hour to negotiate the stairs down to the physical therapy room. It took weeks of working on the stairs until I could move up and down without help but it still took me about thirty minutes.

I began to dream every night about running. Before my accident I ran five to eight miles each day, and I hoped for the day when I could run again.

I loved to run. As long as I could remember, running had been a part of my life. When I joined the army and was assigned to my first duty station in Hawaii I ran six days a week. I think I acquired my love for running while I was working on earning my Expert Infantry

Badge. An EIB is a coveted prize for any soldier and it was a very demanding physical test.

One of those tests is a twelve-mile hike carrying a thirty-pound rucksack up and down the hills in the jungles of Hawaii. The hike was supposed to be completed in three hours or less or you were automatically disqualified.

When I started the hike, I thought I would walk as fast as I could and thought I would finish in plenty of time. At the starting line, the whistle was blown, and a lot of guys took off running. My friend Richard Clark and I started out with a quick pace. It wasn't too long before I found myself running down some of the bigger hills. Then I found myself trying to run up some of the smaller hills. Before I knew it, I was running all the time and passing a lot of my fellow soldiers.

Around the eight-mile point I heard a vehicle approaching from behind, beeping its horn. I turned around to see an army jeep so I moved to the side of the road but kept running. When the jeep was right at my side, I realized it was my Battalion Sergeant Major, and he was yelling at me.

"Laguna! There are only three guys ahead of you. If you beat them and come in first place, I'll give you a three-day pass."

I smiled. "Wow! A three-day pass." I quickly picked up the pace, hoping that I wouldn't burn out before I got to the finish line. A three-day pass was something that was very rewarding, because back in those days we worked five and a half days a week. I must have run another mile before I could see anyone in front of me, and I knew there were at least three more men up there. As I approached the next guy, he seemed to pick up his pace so I quickened my own. It took me about a half a mile to pass him.

There were two and a half miles to go and still two more guys ahead of me. No stretch of the road through the jungle was easy. The whole run was up and down hills, left and right with dense jungle vegetation blocking the view. As I came upon the last mile marker I started to get a little worried, because I hadn't seen the other guys yet.

At that point I decided to start running as fast as I could to the finish line. Somewhere around the last half mile, I came to a hairpin turn going down hill to my left when I saw a quick flash of a guy making the turn. When I saw him, I picked up the pace again and was able to pass him. The next guy was about fifty yards ahead of me, and with only a half-mile to go, hoping for that three-day pass, I ran as hard as I could.

With only one guy to beat and a three-day pass at the finish line, I received another boost of adrenaline. My heart was pounding, and my lungs were burning; however I was determined to beat him. As I approached him we looked at each other, and without saying a word we both began our final dash to the finish line. We stayed with each other stride for stride, and it was just a matter of who could keep up the grueling pace.

The last fifty feet, I looked over to the other guy and smiled and said, "Hang in there. You're doing good." Somewhere I found the strength to press my body a little harder and exerted myself with a little more speed. I pulled away from him just long enough for him to think he didn't have a chance to beat me. It worked. His stride became shorter and I crossed the finish line first.

The Sergeant Major came over to congratulate me and said, "You just earned yourself a three-day pass."

Then he said, "Tomorrow come to my office . . . I want to talk with you."

As requested, the next morning I reported to the Battalion

Sergeant Major. He congratulated me again and told me I could take the three-day pass whenever I wanted. He then said, "That is not why I asked you to come see me."

He continued, "I'm putting together a cross-country track team to represent our battalion and you are now on it. You and the others will be training together every morning. You will not have to report to your company in the morning for physical fitness training."

From that time on, I was a runner. Our team was entered in every race that came up in Hawaii; races like the 140-mile Oahu perimeter run, the twelve-mile Koli Koli Pass run, and many more. As I lay in my hospital room every night, I thought of those days on our battalion track team.

After Doc James saw the progress I made with the crutches, he let me go home for the weekend as a trial to see how things would be with my family providing me with all the medical care I needed. He wanted to see if my family could take care of me.

Getting home wasn't easy. We had a Toyota van, and I didn't realize how much trouble I would have getting in. My legs could not bend as much as was necessary, and I still didn't have the strength to step up and climb in on my own. I tried to just sit on the floor in the back, but I couldn't maneuver myself and get in all the way. Finally, a Chaplain noticed our struggle and came to help me. With his help, I managed to get in the front seat.

When we arrived home, Deonna pulled into our driveway and we went through the same struggle to get me out of the van. And I then faced a new challenge. I had to maneuver myself up the driveway with crutches. The driveway had a slight incline, and as hard as I tried, I just could not make it up the incline. We came up with a new strategy. We wrestled me back into the front seat of the van with my legs hanging out the door, and with all the neighbors watching, Deonna backed out of the driveway and drove right up to the front door as close as she could get. And then I simply stepped onto the porch. With the help of my crutches, I was able to get into the house and into my favorite recliner.

I still needed a lot of attention, because I couldn't just get up and walk with crutches by myself yet. Deonna and the kids had to help me walk to the bathroom, climb upstairs, shower, dress, and to do my exercises. I needed help with everything except sitting in my recliner. Even so, we were happy to be at home together. I went back to the hospital on Monday morning, and they kept me a few weeks longer.

When I was finally discharged from the hospital, my family knew how enthusiastic I was about getting back into shape, so Jamie would take me to the pool for physical therapy quite often. She had worked as a lifeguard before my accident but quit her job to help me recover. It was an indoor pool and usually not many people were there. But when I arrived, what few people were there would take one look at my leg and get out of the pool. I think they were afraid of getting some disease.

It took a lot of work for my family to take care of me. Our oldest daughter, Michelle, had our first grandchild while I was still in the hospital. Michelle came over every day with the baby, and I would lay him on my chest where he would sleep for hours while Michelle did other things around the house. She would help me get to the bathroom during the day and bring me my meals.

Deonna still maintained her busy schedule and went to work

every day. She would get up earlier than normal just to help me get dressed and get downstairs before she left for work. She and the kids sacrificed so much of their time for me without ever once complaining.

The doctors wanted me to have checkups at the burn center in San Antonio every six weeks, so Deonna and I made the trip frequently. The burn doctors were amazed that my leg had survived but were confident I would never be able to use my leg normally again. The tendons and muscles that lifted and dropped my foot from front to back had been severely damaged and burned. The doctors said it was impossible to rebuild the tendons, ligaments, and muscle tissue. They insisted that my leg would be useless to me. That bothered me and I became even more determined to attain my goal.

I never stopped my daily workout in the physical therapy room. When I was in my own bed or in my recliner, I worked with the rubber hose. Because my tendons and muscle tissue were badly burned, I was not able to move my foot and leg in the normal way. My task was to find a new way to move, walk and run with what I had left. After months of exercising my foot with the rubber hose, I had developed my toe muscle. I learned to use my big toe to pick my foot up to walk. That isn't how everyone else walks but it works for me. After months of effort I made some progress, eventually becoming a little more independent.

CHAPTER FOURTEEN
Flying Again

I HAD BEEN HOSPITALIZED FOR four months, and a huge concern had been hovering over me. If I didn't fly at least once every six months, I would lose my flight pay. We couldn't afford to lose the additional flight pay, so as the six-month mark approached, I knew I had to do something.

I called Tom Perkins, a good friend and fellow pilot, and asked him to stop by the next morning and pick me up. I told him I wanted to go out to the flight line and see the guys. I was able to walk with a cane and was doing better, and I was gaining strength every day. I kept my true intentions to myself because I knew if the guys understood what I was up to they wouldn't cooperate.

Tom agreed and said, "Okay, Dan I'll pick you up first thing in the morning."

The next morning, I attempted for the first time in a very long time to put on a pair of army boots. It took a very painful fifteen minutes to get the boot on my still-swollen right foot. When Tom arrived, I was ready to go dressed in my flight suit. When we arrived at the airfield, all the guys were there and happy to greet me. We talked and joked just like before, and I was happy to be reunited with all my good friends.

Sometime later I let the commander know what I was really up to. I said to him, "Sir, I need to find out for myself if I still have what it takes to do my job as a Flight Lead."

When he realized my intentions, he gave me an uncertain look and replied, "Have you received an up-slip?" The term up-slip was slang for a current medical evaluation approving a pilot for flight status.

I said, "No, sir."

He answered, "Well, you know the rules."

I had already prepared for this conversation, and responded, "I don't need an up-slip to fly as a passenger."

He then realized how serious I was. He thought for a moment and said, "You're right."

One of the flight instructors, Tony Renderer, was standing by.

When the commander gave his permission, Tony shrugged his shoulders and said, "Okay, Dan, let's go flying."

Even though I was walking with a cane, I was still considered a Flight Lead in the 160th Special Operations Aviation Regiment. So, out of respect they did what I asked them to do. Two of the guys had to lift me into the bird, because the cockpit was too high for me to step up into. Tony cranked up the bird, and we took off.

There was a part of me, deep down inside that needed to prove I could fly again. I knew there was some emotional stress about the accident, but I didn't know if it would affect my ability to fly to Special Operations standards. I wanted to know if I could still do "surgical shooting" and if I could still do my job. It was important that I find out for myself.

After I got in the air, I asked him to let me take the controls and fly. Tony finally agreed, and I flew for two hours. It felt good. We flew out to Range 29, where the accident happened. I wanted to see and gauge my reaction. Only then would I really know if I could ever again be qualified to do the job I loved.

As we approached Range 29, my stomach was in knots. I made the exact same maneuver at the same target. Again, it felt good. When we landed back on the flight line, there was a shout among the other pilots, and everyone congratulated me.

I turned to Tom Perkins and said, "Will you do me one more favor? Will you take me to the hospital? I'm gonna get an up-slip."

Tom drove me straight to the hospital to see Doc James. I knew the hospital staff very well, so I never called ahead for an appointment. When we reached Dr. James's office, I knocked on the door. He had a patient with him and said he would be with me in a moment. We waited a couple of minutes until the door opened and his patient left.

Doc James said, "Dan, come on in." When I entered his office he said, "Dan, what can I do for you?"

"Doc, I need to get an up-slip."

With compassion in his voice and a slight look of sadness on his face, he said, "Come on Dan. You know you can't fly, not in your condition. It's not possible."

"Sir, I'm serious. I would like you to give me an up-slip."

Dr. James, a good man and by then a good friend, said, "Dan, I can't do that."

I knew he would respond that way, which was why I had to fly first, before I came to see him. I looked directly into his eyes and said, "Doc, I just came back from flying. Perkins can vouch for that."

The surprised doctor looked at me and then at Perkins, as if we were both from another planet.

Perkins said, "Dan just spent two hours with a flight instructor. The guy can fly. He did a demo run on Range 29. It was perfect."

The astonished doctor threw his hands up and agreed to write my up-slip. Having spent the last six months watching my determination, he signed the up-slip and handed it to me with a smile saying, "Keep up the hard work."

I took it back to Flight Operations and was maintained on flight status. I spent the next few months working even harder on my physical therapy routine. Six months after getting my up-slip, I was recovered well enough to go back to work. A total of one year since the accident had gone by.

I knew I had to demonstrate to everyone that I was capable of doing my job as Flight Lead. I had to prove I was not only medically fit, but I could pass a military physical fitness test. The only concern I had on the physical fitness test was the two-mile run. All those nights in the hospital dreaming that I would run again, had motivated me to keep walking and working until I could jog. After I could jog, I began to run short distances, and then longer and longer distances.

It wasn't enough for me to merely complete the run. I wanted to receive the maximum score for my age, so I ran as hard as I could and ended up scoring the maximum for the younger age group. I did not have much healthy cartilage in my left ankle anymore, so running caused some long lasting pain and swelling. I didn't complain, so nobody knew.

I was required to perform hot offloads and uploads in Air Force transport airplanes, which consisted of being able to jump in and out of the Little Bird, pick up a mini gun can of ammunition, which weighed about 125 lbs., and load my own mini-gun and rockets.

There were many other evaluations during which I would have to prove myself, but the one that was the most important to all the operators in the Little Bird Gun Company was to prove I still could plan a major operation, brief it, and conduct a live fire engagement within our very strict standards of performance.

After I completed all the physical tests, I had to qualify as a Flight Lead again. My friend CPT Steve Schiller, the Operations Officer, informed me that Chris Smith was assigned to evaluate me. I had trained Chris to be a Flight Lead about a year earlier.

That night, I was to brief and fly my mission for my Flight Lead evaluation. The weather began to deteriorate. We were in the desert of New Mexico where the weather changed very quickly. On this particular night, the ceiling and visibility were very low. The wind was around thirty knots, which meant I would have to hold a large heading correction.

Prior to starting my brief, Steve and Chris both came to me with concern on their faces.

Chris said, "We can put the evaluation off until tomorrow and see if the weather improves."

I said, "Absolutely not. I'm going to get this evaluation done tonight, even in bad weather."

Because of the gusty winds, this was a difficult evaluation flight, but I completed it exceeding the Task Force standards. Once again, I was authorized to operate as a Flight Lead for TF160. It was a happy day.

The next seven years in the military were just as exciting as the previous twenty-three. Because of my injuries, I had to adapt to a new way of life. I found myself injuring my burned leg quite often. Because I had no feeling in that leg, with even the slightest bump, I often had to pull up my flight suit or pant leg to do a thorough inspection of my skin grafts. Many times the slightest bump was enough to tear a graft, and it would become infected. The doctors warned me about getting an infection in that leg, because it could easily go to the bone.

Even though I was back on active duty, I was required to make visits to the burn ward in San Antonio every six weeks for follow-up care. Those doctor appointments went on for more than a year. On a couple of these trips, I was able to fly my own airplane to Texas.

I had first learned to fly fixed wing when I was in Ft. Bragg back in 1978. I went to a civilian flight school and managed to get my fixed wing rating during the same time frame that I was in Special Forces School. A friend named Pat O'Hara, from the Task Force, was also a fixed wing pilot. Together, we bought a Cessna 310, dual engine airplane.

Dr. Barrillo was my doctor in the Burn Unit in San Antonio. On subsequent visits to the burn ward, each time Dr. Barrillo saw me, he would immediately tell me to take my pants off so he could show me off to some of his colleagues and other patients.

He would tell them, "Look at this guy. He was told he would always have to walk with some kind of walking device and that he would never be able to fly again. Now look at him. He walks without a cane, and he flew his own airplane here."

After I was paraded around the burn ward, I was able to visit with some of the burn patients. I always enjoyed these visits, because they gave me an opportunity to encourage people who were alone and discouraged by their injuries. It seemed important for me to give something back to the medical profession for all the unselfish time and consideration they showed me during the most trying days of my life. Later when I retired from the military, and flew for the University of Utah hospital, I was able to visit and encourage burn patients there as well.

CHAPTER FIFTEEN
More Surgery

I FELL BACK INTO THE same routine of planning and rehearsing for missions. Deonna and I decided to postpone retirement, because I still needed medical care and were unsure whether I could be employed outside of the military or not. It was a financial decision.

The following year, our unit was doing some specialized training in Poland. I was the officer in charge (OIC) of the Little Bird Company on that deployment. I was sent to Poland with an advanced team to determine the feasibility of a Task Force Deployment to work with Poland's GROM unit. Poland's GROM unit is the equivalent to our Special Operations units.

Our advance team traveled by convoy to many different locations, and it was interesting to see some of the poverty-stricken areas, still suffering from when the communist Soviet Union had a strong hold in the country. One of the more interesting nights was spent in a fourteenth century castle, recently renovated as a bed and breakfast inn. After I checked in, I went exploring and found an access door that led to the attic. Just like a little kid, curiosity got the better of me. As I pushed on the stuck door, I imagined a scene right out of the movies, where the attic was covered with spider webs and dust. I explored around the dusty old furniture in an ancient room that was hundreds of years old.

When we arrived back in the U.S., I immediately started to plan our units' return to Poland. Three weeks later, we were deployed to Poland to work and train with the GROM.

The four weeks of training with the GROM was a success. We were able to share some of our tactical expertise and see how they planned and executed a Special Ops mission. It was a lot of hard work, but it was also a lot of fun.

As we were packing to leave, our guys and the GROM guys decided to have a BBQ. To my surprise, the BBQ turned out to be more formal than anticipated. We didn't know that the GROM unit had invited the Prime Minister of Poland to our BBQ. When the Prime Minister showed up, we were all in military formation. The Prime Minister addressed us all and thanked us for coming to Poland and training side-by-side with their elite GROM unit.

He then called Dave Ray and me to come up to where he was. I did not have a clue what was going on, but this became one of the highlights in my military career. Dave Ray and I were awarded GROM status by the Prime Minister, with all power and authority that comes with being a GROM member. We became the only two Americans who were card-carrying members of the GROM force.

The day after training with the GROM, the Special Operations doctor noticed that I was walking with a little bit of a limp and said, "Hey, Dan, take off your flight suit so I can examine your leg."

He knew of my helicopter accident a couple years earlier and about some of the ongoing leg pain I was dealing with every day.

I did as he asked, and he brought out this protractor-looking device to measure my legs.

After he did so, he said, "Your left leg is approximately twenty degrees verus. That meant that my leg bowed inward from the knee to the ankle about twenty degrees too much.

He specialized in orthopedic surgery and spent a few minutes poking and prodding and then said with a voice of confidence, "I can fix that. When we get back to the States, you come and see me. I'll have you walking straight again."

In order to fix my leg, the doctor would have to operate and re-break my leg and attach an external fixator device. This was a device that looked like a bicycle rim with spokes (pins). Each pin attached to one side of the rim and went through the bone of the leg and attached to the other side of the rim.

Shortly after I got home from our trip to Poland, I was brought to the Delta Compound to get with this doctor, who had performed the same surgery on a Special Ops guy who was wounded in Mogadishu, Somalia.

Deonna accompanied me to Ft. Bragg where I had the surgery. She had to learn how to take care of the pin sites so they would not get infected. I had sixteen pins drilled completely through my leg bone, which created thirty-two pin sites that Deonna had to clean twice a day.

I was required to turn a small screw about a quarter of a turn once a day. By turning this screw, it would separate the bone and not allow it to heal completely. This would lengthen the bone about three fourths of an inch over a six-month period.

While I was in the hospital after the surgery, still in the recovery room, the nurse came in and asked, "Sir, how are you feeling?"

Still groggy from the anesthesia, I said to her, "The top of my left foot feels like it is burning."

She replied, "But you didn't have surgery on your foot."

I insisted, "My foot is burning."

She took off the ace bandage that was wrapped from the bottom of my foot to my knee.

She asked, "How did you get burned?"

I told her, "A couple years ago I was in a helicopter accident."

She said, "No, how did you get this burn?"

I sat up slightly to see what she was talking about. The entire top of my left foot was blistered. I told her it wasn't there when I came to the hospital, and she became upset and ran out of the room.

She quickly came back with a doctor, and they examined the new burn I now had on my left foot. Without saying a word, they stood there with puzzled looks on their faces. They came to the conclusion that I had a third degree chemical burn from the foot being wrapped too tight with an ace bandage after they had used Betadine to clean the skin before surgery.

The breaks in both legs from the helicopter accident caused a lot of damage and scar tissue, and I no longer had cartilage between the bones in my ankles. The doctors told me I would most likely develop arthritis in my ankles. It took a couple of very painful years of walking on my ankles to break up the scar tissue, and it was still painful, so I had to have steroid shots in my ankles every six months for about two years.

This was my last major surgery, and it has been successful. After this procedure was completed and healed six months later, I was able to walk with a lot less pain.

CHAPTER SIXTEEN
Operations In Baghdad

I STARTED WORKING IN IRAQ for Blackwater in September of 2004. As all Blackwater contractors do, I headed for Iraq with an overnight stop in Amman, Jordan. Sometimes after thirty hours of traveling, depending on where you left from in the United States, it is a well-deserved stop. The next morning, ten of us made the two-hour flight on a private Blackwater airplane from Amman to the Baghdad International Airport.

After takeoff, everyone would try to get settled in for the long flight either by plugging into their iPods, working on their computers, or just taking a nap. Once we entered Iraq's airspace, we were issued weapons just in case the aircraft went down en route. Upon arrival over Baghdad International Airport air space, the pilot began his spiral descent for landing. The descent was so aggressive that by the time we were on the ground, some of the guys were sick, but that was the best way to avoid enemy ground fire.

Every night after supper and our nightly briefing, the chief pilot and I would go out and sit next to the hangar to wait for the show to begin. We called it Baghdad TV. Around sunset, the insurgents would shoot anywhere from two to four rockets into the Green Zone. Many times the rockets would land right on LZ Washington, where we lived. Sometimes it would get really comical watching guys who had never been in that type of environment. They would start running for a bunker and end up hurting themselves running for cover. We would sit in our chairs and watch the show. It may have seemed crude to some people, but that was the kind of humor you'd find among warriors.

On one of our missions, we were providing overhead security for a ground team when we suddenly came under fire by insurgents. We could hear a lot of automatic gunfire from the ground. Getting shot at was a frequent occurrence, so we always flew with two pilots so if one was shot, the other pilot could fly the helicopter. On this particular day, the other pilot with me took a bullet to the foot. I took the controls and flew him to the hospital. Fortunately, his injury was not serious.

On January 10, 2005, we had just finished escorting one of our ground teams. As we shut down our helicopters and waited for our next mission, we could hear gunfire coming from behind the Embassy. A hasty plan was made, and then both crews jumped back into their helicopters. I flew directly to the Fourteenth of July Bridge, a well-known landmark, and turned left along the Tigris River to see if we could find where the firing was coming from and assist as needed.

The other helicopter was to fly directly to the same bridge, turn right, and do the same. It was not more than thirty seconds after we had turned left from the bridge that I could see a squad-size army patrol pinned down by automatic fire coming from a building that looked like an apartment complex. The insurgents were on the top floor of a four-story apartment building shooting at the army patrol, which was now in the prone position taking cover.

I made a quick assessment. With the other pilot at the controls we decided to fly down the street at the same level as the insurgents shooting from the fourth floor. We brought the helicopter in from the backside of the apartment building so we would have the element of surprise.

As we flew around the corner of the apartment building at the same level of the windows from where the insurgents were shooting, Mark Caracci, a former Navy SEAL, and I stood ready with our M4s prepared to return fire. It was a risky maneuver, close to the ground and to the buildings. We were extremely exposed to their automatic fire setting on the left side of the helicopter, but it was the only way we could suppress the insurgents so the army patrol could get up from their pinned-down position. As the insurgents came into view, we could see them shooting at the army patrol. Mark and I opened fire on them, and then the surprised insurgents stopped shooting at the army patrol and started shooting at us. That was the plan.

We both went through several magazines of ammunition engaging the insurgents, exposed to their automatic fire, but we were never hit. When the pinned army patrol saw that the insurgents fire was redirected at the helicopter, they jumped up and ran into the building. With us providing cover fire, the U.S. Army patrol was able to make it safely into the building where the insurgents were firing from and tactically make their way to the fourth floor, capturing all the insurgents.

As we flew around to the back of the building, we saw two of the insurgents trying to escape out of a back window. Mark quickly changed their mind with a few shots, so they jumped back in and were captured. There were nine insurgents in the building, and four tested positive for TNT, which meant they were making bombs.

On my second trip back to Iraq, my brother Art had just arrived in Iraq with the California National Guard. Art would often fly into LZ (Landing Zone) Washington on passenger transport missions. Whenever he had some free time waiting on passengers, he would come over to visit with me. Each time we talked, I tried to recruit him over to Blackwater Aviation.

Art told me, "When I leave Iraq I never want to see this hellhole again." I told him if he ever changed his mind to let me know. During the year Art spent in Iraq, we were able to spend some quality time together; a lot of the guys in Blackwater got to know him as well.

I spent a lot of time going back and forth to Iraq. Working in Baghdad those first two years, I had numerous opportunities to see the good we in Blackwater Aviation were able to contribute to Operation Iraqi Freedom. I can remember many times while we were doing our jobs, providing overhead security, that we were able to save a life of a coalition force member.

On one of our U.S. Ambassador's convoy security moves, we had just departed a place where he had a very important meeting and arrived at the gate into the Green Zone when we heard and felt the concussion of a very large explosion. The explosion was very close to where my helicopter was orbiting, with the Ambassador safely in the Green Zone; I immediately flew to the location of the explosion to see if someone was going to need our help. The location was only seconds away. As I arrived overhead, I could see an IED had taken out an army Humvee. There were four soldiers lying outside their Humvee. It was obvious that the soldiers had been blown out of the Humvee by the IED. I quickly landed the helicopter within ten feet of them and told my door gunner, Paul Simpson, a medic, to assess their injuries and see if we need to Medevac anyone to the hospital.

With the helicopter on the ground and running, ready for a quick takeoff, Ron Johnson (Cat Daddy) and I sat there feeling uncomfortable out in the open, waiting for Paul to do his assessment. The other door gunner was pulling security to our rear, and Ron took the controls so I could pull security on the left side of the helicopter. If we had not been there the wounded would likely have been killed by the insurgents. Within thirty seconds of being on the ground, I observed an old Iraqi man jump up from behind a four-foot high hedge bush about seventy five feet away and then immediately disappear. I pointed my M4 in his direction just in case he jumped back up with a weapon. When he popped back up, he had a little girl in his arms and started to walk toward the helicopter. I raised my M4 and my left hand, trying to motion him to stop. I kept waving my hand, trying to get his attention for him to stop and not come any closer, but he ignored my plea.

At the same time I flipped my M4 from safe to fire. I did not want to take the chance that he may have been involved with the IED attack. There was the possibility of him being a suicide bomber carrying the little girl as a cover. I came within a couple of seconds of shooting him when suddenly I noticed an army soldier running toward him, trying to get him to stop as well.

The soldier had his weapon pointed at the Iraqi man and little girl as he approached them. When the soldier was able to get them to stop, they were only about twenty feet away. I could see that the old Iraqi man was crying with the little girl in his arms. The soldier escorted them closer to the helicopter toward me, and when they were within a few feet I could see the little girl had been a casualty of the explosion. Her injuries were awful. Her right leg hung by a small amount of skin, and she had a very large abdomen wound with some of her intestines exposed.

About the same time Paul was loading one of the most seriously injured soldiers into the back of the Little Bird, the old man was motioning that he wanted to put the little girl in the helicopter with the soldier. I made a quick assessment of the little girl and knew she was not going to survive. She appeared to be dead already. The decision I had to make that day-- to leave that little girl there -- was one of the hardest decisions I have ever had to make, but it really came down to taking her or the soldier. Later that day, I found out the little girl died as we took off, and if I had taken her instead of the soldier, the soldier would have died waiting for an army Medevac. The decision I made still haunts me, even though I feel I made the right decision. To this day, I can close my eyes and still see that little girl's face. That sweet little girl who like so many other innocent ones, was killed by militants who had no concern for the kind of suffering they caused.

Oct 3, 2007 started off as a normal day with us providing aerial security support for convoys going into the Red Zone. You could hear the usual explosions in the surrounding areas of Baghdad. Around 10 AM I received a call from the U.S. Embassy requesting a QRF (Quick Reaction Force) mission. I was advised that the Polish Ambassador's convoy was just hit with an IED in a complex attack in the Red Zone. I was then informed the U.S. military would not be able to help because of the very narrow streets, buildings, and many other obstacles that would prevent them from landing their helicopters. Also, the military's response time to help was much greater than ours; I could have a team in the air in the local Baghdad area in less than five minutes. As I put my crew together, I had a team that just finished a mission in the Red Zone. I gave them all a quick brief of the situation, and within a couple of minutes, we were airborne, headed to the ambush site. It took us about three minutes to get to the Polish Ambassador's location. Upon arrival, I could see the devastation from the IED and complex attack. Because of the narrow streets, I had my big helicopter, a Bell 412, orbit overhead while I put two Little Birds down in the street to evacuate the Polish Ambassador and the wounded. Polish Ambassador Pietrzyk and one of his bodyguards were the first to be evacuated. The second Little Bird flew out two more wounded.

This was only one of numerous times we were called upon to conduct a QRF mission in the Red Zone to help a coalition force. We were called upon to help regularly because of our quickness to respond to the call for help.

About three and a half months later, after his recovery in the hospital in Poland, the Polish Ambassador returned to Baghdad and called me, asking if we could meet to talk. I told him I would be happy to meet with him and that I was surprised to hear he was back in Baghdad so soon.

The Ambassador arrived at LZ Washington about an hour later. We sat in the hangar and talked about his rescue on October 3, 2007. He showed me his burns, and I showed him mine so I could let him see what they would look like in a year or more after they had some time to heal.

Filled with emotion and his voice cracking, he kept telling me over and over how grateful he was for my saving his life. I could see he had weeks of swelling emotion in side of him and could not wait to thank his rescue team in person.

In Poland he had extensive surgery and medical care, and was now returning to war-torn Baghdad, Iraq. Many thought he would never return. I told him we were happy to help him and glad that his recovery was going well.

He replied, "Dan, thank you. Thank you very much. You saved my life."

I knew he was sincere, because he said it with tears in his eyes. After we talked about the rescue, he handed me a piece of paper with a list of names. He asked if I would confirm that the names on the list were those individuals who had been part of his rescue. I mentioned there were a couple of names missing from his list. He gave me the list and asked me to update it with correct spellings and to e-mail it back as soon as I was able. He then explained that he and the country of Poland were extremely thankful for us in the rescue of their Ambassador and that they were going to honor each person with a medal.

He said because I was the Flight Lead for the rescue mission and the Blackwater Aviation Program Manager, I would receive Poland's Silver Star and the others would receive Poland's Bronze Star for heroism in his rescue.

I again thanked him and said, "Mr. Ambassador, that is not necessary. We are just happy that we were able to help and that you are safe."

As he was leaving, he gave me a hug and said, "You and your men are heroes. You gave me a second life."

The next day, one of his GROM guys met with me and asked if I could give him the exact location where they had been hit with the IED and the location where we had landed to pick up the Ambassador. I printed out a picture from Google Earth with the coordinates marking each location. A few hours later, I ran into the Polish Ambassador at the U.S. Embassy (Saddam Hussein's former palace), and he gave me the personal invitations for all my guys to attend the award ceremony at the Baghdad Polish Embassy on January 25, 2008.

Ambassador Pietrzyk then asked, "How would you like to see Poland?"

I said, "I would love to go back to Poland again."

He looked at me with a surprise on his face and said, "Again?"

I said, "Yes, Mr. Ambassador, I have been there before."

At that moment his GROM bodyguard bent down and whispered in his ear. From the look on his face he has just been told that I was one of the two Americans who had been awarded GROM status. He then stated that I should come to Poland and bring my wife; I just said it would be an honor for us to go to Poland.

On January 25, 2008 around 4:45 PM, we had a PSD (Personal Security Detail) team with their Suburban's pull up in front of the hangar on LZ Washington. All the awardees were going to get the full VIP treatment. Everyone loaded up in the vehicles. We were instructed to be at the Polish Embassy no later than 5:00 PM, before U.S. Ambassador Crocket arrived. Polish Ambassador Pietrzyk and his bodyguards met us upon our arrival at the Polish Embassy. The Polish Embassy was in the Red Zone until the attack on the Polish Ambassador on October 3, 2007. For the life of me, I could not figure out why any country would put their diplomats in such a hostile living environment.

We were escorted into a small room where the ceremony was to be held. Shortly after we arrived, U.S. Ambassador Crocket arrived, and later, General Petraeus. Before the award ceremony started, I was able to spend some time talking with both Ambassadors. We were told that General Petraeus would be arriving late because of prior engagements. Polish Ambassador Pietrzyk decided to start the award ceremony without General Petraeus present. Ambassador Pietrzyk started with a speech he had prepared in which he gave me a copy.

Here are his remarks:

"Blessed are the peacemakers: for they shall be called the children of God (Matthew 5:9)

YOUR EXCELLENCY,

Ladies & Gentlemen,

I am very proud to be here with you, specially with you!

That's not secret – I'm here because of you, the people, who are proudly carrying the name "BLACK WATERS." Because of you, the people who without hesitations, without fear came by air to help me and my colleagues, to prove that we are sharing the same values, that the friendship is not empty sound. Before the 3rd of October, I didn't realized how many friends around the world I have. And you are among them.

Many peoples, also the high ranking in my country, asked me many times: WHY? Why are you going back to Baghdad? Today, with permission given by your Ambassador, He, Ryan Crocker, I invited you – the first distinguished guests, in order to tell you in the presence of your superior: I KNOW THE CORRECT ANSWER! I'm here to tell to you THANKS FOR THE SECOND LIFE! My family, my wife Anna Alicja, both my sons Jan and Nicolas, and myself we will always remember Americans who came in few decisive minutes to the proper place. You were at the very beginning of my long way to recovery. That beginning I remember very well AND WILL NEVER BE FORGOTTEN. After being out of conscious for long two weeks, when I opened the eyes I realized ...My government by ministries of Foreign Affairs MR. Radek SIKORSKI and Minister of Defense Mr. Bogdan Klich has decided to express gratitude to the members of rescue team.

On behalf of my government let me to hand LETTERS OF APPRECIATION and MEDALS OF THE POLISH ARMED FORCES."

As he spoke those words, you could see the emotion build up in him. Filled with emotion, he paused a couple of times to wipe away tears before he completed his remarks.

At the end of his remarks, he said, "We will commence with the awards by bringing Dan Laguna up first."

As I took those few steps up to where he was standing, my thoughts quickly returned to October 3, 2007, when I led our Quick Reaction Force (QRF) to his rescue and thought what might have happened if we had been just a couple of minutes later.

When I stood there as he pinned the Silver Star on me, he again thanked me, saying, as he gave me a big hug, "You gave me my second life."

I said, "Sir, it was meant to be."

The rest of my guys were brought up one at a time to receive their Bronze Stars. Shortly after all the awards were given out, General Petraeus showed up, congratulated each person, and gave each of us his coin. On the coin, it stated "For Excellence in Combat." After all the formalities were done, I talked with General Petraeus for about twenty minutes.

I was informed later that this was the first Silver Star ever awarded to an American since WWII. What an honor. Here is a list of men and the medals they received that night:

SILVER STAR
Dan Laguna   Flight Lead/Little Bird and Aviation Program Manager

BRONZE STAR
Frank Paul   Flight Lead/Little Bird

Rick Stout	Flight Lead/ Little Bird
Abe Bronn	Flight Lead/ Little Bird
John Nussbaum	Co-Pilot/ Little Bird
Paul Chopra	Co-Pilot/ Little Bird
Dick Aanerud	Lead Pilot/Bell 412
Hoyt Fraiser	Lead Pilot/Bell 412
Brian Perlis	Door Gunner
Clint Matoon	Door Gunner
Josh Kinny	Door Gunner
Brian O'Malley	Door Gunner
Daniel Pray	Door Gunner
Wilson McKiethan	Door Gunner
Nathan Pohl	Door Gunner
Anthony Sanganetti	Tactical Operations Center
Scott Bruggemann	Tactical Operations Center
Ali Murjan	Tactical Operations Center

CHAPTER SEVENTEEN
More Memories of Art

THE DAY OF MY BROTHER'S funeral was one of the hardest days of my life, other than the day he died. After the funeral and luncheon, family and friends met at the American Legion. The mood at the American Legion Hall was much more uplifting. We were all feeling better, and everyone brought up funny stories about Art. It felt good to laugh and remember the good times.

My sister Mona reminded us of the time Art was landing his plane but forgot to put down his landing gear. He was shocked to find his aircraft sliding down the runway on its belly, causing very costly repairs. The Blackwater door gunners were at the hall, and laughed louder than anyone at the story about their old boss.

Art often flew to air shows and frequently would run into someone who knew me. One time he flew to a place he'd never been and was checking into the hotel when someone came up to him and asked, "Are you Dan Laguna?"

Art went straight to his room and called me in the middle of the night to ask, "Is there any place I can go where people don't know you?"

This happened to him so often that his wife said she was going to have a T-shirt made that said, "I'm not Dan." I was happy we had the kind of relationship where he could call in the middle of the night to poke fun at me.

I told everyone the story about a time when I arranged for the California National Guard to train with us. At the time, our brother Milo was Art's crew chief and they were the crew assigned to train with us. The training mission called for a helicopter crew to land on a very small clearing of an eighteen hundred-foot peak. The landing spot was barely big enough for the skids to land on, and Art got the assignment. Art was able to land his helicopter on the mountain peak where not many pilots would feel comfortable landing in such a small area. Art and Milo jumped out and located the targets we were to shoot that night while they were sitting on the hillside. Their job was to place a laser beam on the target we were to shoot, and then I would climb up, see the target that was being marked, and fire mini-gun and rockets.

The high peak had a very steep cliff on one side, and that was the side from where I approached the target. Flying very fast, I would fly nearly vertical, then nose the helicopter over, lock onto the target, and fire away. We did this maneuver all day long.

On the first run of the night firing, I decided to rattle them a little bit. I approached their position on the hilltop from behind and instead of firing from a distance, I locked onto the target from directly over their heads. At the sound of the mini-gun and rockets firing exactly over their heads, they were surprised and nearly fell down the cliff, scrambling to get away from the noise and hot brass. We laughed about that for years.

After a couple of hours of storytelling and laughs, we all decided to go home. Before we left, the President of Presidential Airways went to his car and brought out some Blackwater souvenirs and T-shirts. He gave them all to me to distribute to Art's daughters at a later time. Deonna and I drove to our hotel. It had been a long, emotional day, and it had been a long week, too. The funeral was over and I felt like I could unwind now.

Just as we arrived at our room, I received a phone call from one of the guys in Baghdad. It was a good friend who was on the ground team the day Art and the others had been killed. I knew him well and knew what kind of soldier he was. This was a former Spec Ops guy who was a tough guy doing a tough job, but on this day he broke down in tears.

This good man said through his tears, "We should have done better for you. I feel like these guys died because I didn't do my job."

I was surprised by his words.

"You did everything you could. This was not your fault."

He insisted he should have done more. "I'm so sorry I let you down. We just ran out of ammo. We should've done more to help."

I tried to comfort him. "That was the biggest shootout we've ever had in Baghdad. We had no way of knowing about the attack. I know you did everything you could."

The massive amount of gunfire from nearly a thousand insurgents forced the guys to use much more ammunition than they were typically carrying. During the firefight, some teams had to break off to obtain more ammunition, and that was when the shoot-down occurred. Art and his crew were shot down while this guy was away getting resupplied. He felt a lot of guilt about that. We talked for thirty minutes, and I assured him that I was proud of him and his job performance that day.

That phone call brought me back into a melancholy mood.

As I lay back on the bed, Deonna reminded me, "Art's in a better place. He's happy and at peace."

I knew she was right. Our faith had been a huge part of our lives and had made all the difference during other times like this.

I hadn't slept much for the last week, so I was tired and began to drift away to sleep. A thousand scenes replayed in my memory. A lot had happened during my many years in the military. More often than I could even remember, my life had been in danger, yet there I was safe and sound with Deonna at my side.

CHAPTER EIGHTEEN
Miracles

I THINK A LOT ABOUT the various situations where my life was in grave danger. In every circumstance, I was saved, often in miraculous ways. The day my brother and friends were killed, I was in a helicopter so badly crippled that we were forced to make an emergency landing. Bullet holes riddled the rotor blades, fuselage, and much of the electronic equipment, yet all of us were spared. I didn't think the helicopter could fly any longer in its battered condition.

While we were on the ground at the Ministry of Health, inspecting the damage to the helicopter, we were about to be attacked by dozens of insurgents, and we had a helicopter that had just been shot down and was in very bad condition. Yet a helicopter that should never have flown again started up and flew us to safety.

As a new pilot in Hawaii, I was flying a helicopter that was starting to make a strange sound. I didn't know that the rotor blades were separating, but I listened to what some would call a "gut feeling."

I called it "listening to the whisperings of the Holy Ghost." Luckily, I acted on that feeling, because it was in me to think that I could go just a little farther, that it would be okay, I could make it.

As a new skydiver, I avoided death by a mere second or two, maybe less. Some may say that it was luck, but I distinctly remember being so panicked when all of a sudden I felt a calm come over me, which helped me to think clearly and do what I needed to do to save myself.

In Panama, my family and I nearly went over a cliff, which would have been certain death. Our car managed to hit the only tree big enough to stop us from going over the cliff. I doubt very much that was a coincidence either.

While in Iraq during Desert Storm, I flew to safety during a terrible dust storm while another helicopter pilot that same night decided to try to make it back despite the dust storm, because he was carrying a badly injured soldier. They didn't make it; they crashed just prior to the runway, killing everyone onboard. I spent the night out of radio contact and waited for the weather to clear before I went back.

In Mogadishu, I narrowly escaped a mortar round that severely wounded my good friends and killed at least one other soldier.

My survival the night of my helicopter accident was a long string of miracles. Deonna had a very bad feeling and knew something was wrong. She called me repeatedly to warn me about flying that day. I should have listened to her.

The extent of my injuries with both legs severely broken, broken ribs, punctured lungs, and severe burns to 31 percent of my body would make it *impossible* for anyone to climb out of a burning helicopter on their own, let alone get to a safe distance from the burning, exploding helicopter. Remember, the helicopter rested on its side with me on the topside, held in only by my seatbelt or harness. When I released my seatbelt, I should have fallen into Carlos, where the flames were coming from. I would have had to climb up and out to save myself. With my injuries it would have been *impossible.*

I was soaked with JP4, the helicopter fuel, and was surrounded by intense flames. I should have lit up like a torch.

The Medevac helicopter just happened to be in the area that night and was able to respond within minutes. From the time of the accident to the time Deonna received that fateful phone call was approximately thirty minutes.

I received a Bishop's blessing the night of my accident. Many who are not LDS do not understand this, but a blessing is based on the faith of both the person giving it and the person receiving it.

There was a big controversy about the type of boots I was wearing that night. Special Ops units were not required to adhere to the same dress standards as the regular army. I was not wearing a full leather boot as the regular army required. I was wearing boots with Cordura and leather. Cordura was quick drying and <u>NOT</u> flame retardant. If I had been wearing a full leather boot, according to the burn doctors, I most likely would have lost my right foot. The leather kept reigniting, causing my toes and Achilles tendon to be burned. Those were the areas on the boot that were leather. The part of the boot made of Cordura, protected most of my foot by dissipating the heat from the fire.

Deonna left her meeting at the very moment the accident occurred. I don't think that was coincidence. I feel that she and I were so in tune with each other that she subconsciously knew something very bad had just happened. She felt those bad vibes all day long and called me many times to warn me. Some might have called them premonitions.

While in the Guest House in Texas, Deonna received a prompting that told her the same thing three times, "Leave the room." She admitted that she didn't recognize it as a prompting until she actually acted on it and went downstairs and saw a good friend checking out of the Guest House. If it had been just a few moments later, she would have completely missed him and not known he had been there, and I would not have received the support and many blessings that he gave me over the next several weeks.

The doctors didn't expect me to survive at all, let alone keep my charred leg. My religious commitments to God have been the reason for my successes and survival. I have strived to live as an honorable man, doing my best to follow the example of our Lord and Savior. As a Mormon, I made promises in the temple to live the commandments and serve others. I wear the temple garments, as an outward commitment of those inner desires to do good wherever I go.

The fact that I was protected from being burned by the undergarments caused some stir among the guys in my unit. Some time after the accident, Colonel Doug Brown, my commanding officer, now a retired four-star General, asked me where to find this special underwear, because he wanted all of his flight crews to wear the same material.

I said, "Sir, that's not going to work."

He protested, "Why not? It worked for you."

I had to explain to him, "Sir, it's not the cloth. It's the faith."

Months after I was out of the hospital, both of the Task Force medics who had saved my life that night, Robert Kofahl and Paul Stevenson, came by to visit me. They asked if they could ask me a personal question about the night of the accident.

I said, "Sure, no problem. What is it?"

They wanted to know why I had fought them when they had tried to cut off my long white underwear, because I had acted like it was a life or death situation. I just told them it was something to do with my religion, and I would explain it to them someday. I really didn't know how to explain it to them.

About a year later, Paul Stevenson saw my wife and me in the Post Exchange (PX) and said, "Dan, I have always had this unanswered question in the back of my mind. You were soaked in fuel, on fire, and burned everywhere except where your long, white underwear was covering your body. I can't understand why."

I tried my best to explain it to him. I told him I was LDS, some knew us as Mormons. Paul had a puzzled look on his face.

I said, "That long, white underwear you are talking about is a religious garment I wear for spiritual reasons. If we live worthily, the garments will protect us spiritually as well as physically."

I don't think he understood what I was trying to tell him, but we spoke a while longer before he left and went on with his day. He walked away with the same puzzled look I had seen on others who had tried to understand.

CHAPTER NINETEEN
Another Happy Day

The morning after Art's funeral, Deonna and I stopped at Mom's house to say good-bye. She knew I was going back to Baghdad and had a concerned look. We hugged, said our good-byes, and left for the airport.

Upon landing in Salt Lake City, good friends of ours, Steve and Athalie Yeiter, picked us up and saw that we were both in a somber mood. In a day or two, I would be leaving again for Iraq, so Deonna was beginning to feel concerned. We spoke little on our trip from the airport to our home in North Salt Lake, both consumed by our thoughts.

About a mile from home, Steve, who was driving, pointed to something that I would have failed to notice. There was a marquis sign with a scrolling message: "Welcome Home, Dan Laguna." Beyond the sign were American flags on both sides of the road for the entire mile to our house. As we pulled into our driveway, there were about a hundred friends and neighbors there to welcome us home. It was a surprising and emotional scene. We climbed out of the car and noticed three different television news crews among the group, and then we heard the sounds of two news helicopters flying overhead.

Our house sat on the edge of a bluff that overlooks the city. Two of our good friends, Julie and Nevin Graves, started a donation drive in our neighborhood to obtain enough money to build a monument in honor of Art and the others killed that day. They planned to construct the monument and flagpole at the edge of the bluff in our backyard. When Colonial Flag in Sandy, Utah, heard about the plans, they not only volunteered to install the flagpole, but they paid for it as well.

We were walked around to the side of the house, and the beautiful flag and monument came into view. It was a breathtaking scene, and it was so very appreciated. Tears were on every cheek. Soon, the neighbors made their way home, and the wonderful scene was shown on the television stations that evening.

As we prepared to go to sleep that night like every night we're together, Deonna and I knelt by the side of our bed and thanked God for his love and mercy.

A few days later, I returned to Baghdad and tried to immerse myself in my work to escape the memories and pain of Art's death.

A few days after I was back in Baghdad, Dr. Condoleezza Rice, Secretary of State, showed up in Baghdad. I heard through Ambassador Zalmay Khalilzad that Dr. Rice wanted to speak to me. I was able to have a couple of private minutes with Dr. Rice.

The first thing she said was, "Dan, I am so sorry to hear about your brother, Arthur."

I thanked her for her sincere comments about Art and then introduced Dr. Rice to the Blackwater Aviation guys. Dr. Rice talked to the guys for a few moments, thanking them for what they did, and then we had a photo session with her. I had other opportunities to meet VIPs like her while working in Baghdad. I was also able to meet President Bush on one of his visits to Baghdad.

After that rotation back in Iraq was over, I was ready to go home and be with Deonna. There were so many things to work out in my head still, and Deonna was a very big comfort for me. She understood my feelings and thoughts and would reassure me when needed.

There was a time early in my career when I decided I would leave each duty station with a change for the positive. I wanted to leave my mark everywhere I went, and I hoped to change any negative attitudes of others around me. People who were negative and complained about everything would ultimately affect the attitudes of others around them.

I decided one day I would try to change the attitudes of others by greeting everyone with, "It's another happy day!"

I said it so often and with such enthusiasm that it started catching on. Repeating the phrase made me feel better, and that positive attitude spread to those around me. Before long, everyone knew me for that phrase, and they began saying it. It became a game of sorts, and guys would try to beat me to the punch line or say it before I did. We would laugh and we all felt better.

I really tried to live by that motto. As time went on and I experienced truly horrible events in my life, I could do one of two things: let the experience affect me negatively and feel sorry for myself, blaming others and God, or I could see things in a more positive light and have *another happy day.*

Even through the deaths of several friends in the military, family members, and men who worked with me in Blackwater, I have strived to see things in a positive way. Death is part of life. Although I know everyone has to die, sometimes it isn't easy to accept it. I've learned to focus on truth, not sorrow to get through it.

My religious beliefs get me through the worst times. I know that we all return to God, our Father in Heaven. He and only He controls when we return. I truly believe that a righteous man or woman will not die until it is his or her time assigned by God. I have evidence of that in my own life. I don't believe that just because people weren't saved from some awful situation and died, that they were not righteous. I believe it was their time to return to our Father in Heaven where we all came from.

I have been saved numerous times from death. I know that for a fact. That is why I do what I do for a living. I want to make a difference in this world the only way I know how. I know I will see all my friends, family, and loved ones again someday. We will all meet in a much better place than this world. God is a loving God who sees the bigger picture. We have to have faith in Him that He will do what is best for each of us. We are here on this earth to gain experiences that will help us grow and become better people. We will all miss our loved ones when they pass to the other side. When we grieve their passing, we are really grieving for ourselves, because we will not see them again in this life and will miss them. I wish everyone would understand the way I do, that we will all be together again.

So, to my fallen brothers, family, and friends who have already gone to the other side, I say, "God be with you till we meet again."

APPENDIX
Arthur Laguna
10 Aug 1954 - 23 Jan 2007

ARTHUR (ART) LAGUNA ENLISTED IN the United States Army in June 1972 as an infantryman. After serving six years in the infantry Art left active duty and joined the California National Guard as a helicopter crew chief/mechanic. In September 1982 Art was accepted into the Army's Flight School Program. Upon graduating from Flight School and fulfilling a childhood dream, Art quickly became one of the Army's best pilots. Art is a graduate of the Army's Instrument Examiner Course, Instructor Pilot's Course,

Army Aviation Safety Course, Maintenance Test Pilot Course and the Army's Fixed Wing Course.

Art has served in combat in Bosnia and Iraq with the United States Military as a Lead Pilot. After serving in Iraq and in the United States Army for thirty-four years with distinction and valor, Art was looking for his next challenge and joined the Blackwater Aviation Team. Upon graduating from Blackwater training he immediately deployed to Baghdad Iraq. Art was able to become a Bell 412 (Big Bird) Lead Pilot quicker than anyone has and was working on becoming a MD 530 (Little Bird) Lead Pilot.

Art once said, working with Blackwater was the highlight in his career thus far. He felt like he made it to the Super Bowl.

Prior to Art being shot down, he had received an award for responding to a military unit that was hit by an Improvised Explosive Device (IED) causing many casualties. Because of Art's quick thinking and response, he and his team were able to save lives that day.

Art died on January 23, 2007 in combat doing what he did best, helping others. For all those that knew Art, he was a HERO.

TALK GIVEN BY DAN AT ART'S FUNERAL SERVICE

I was asked to talk a little about Art today. But before I can speak about Art, you need to know the names of the BRAVE MEN (WARRIORS) that fought and died in combat beside him.

Ron (Catdaddy) Johnson, a former Night Stalker, a man that had seen combat many times in his military career.

Steven ("G MAN") Gernet

Casey (ROOSTER) Casavant

Shane (WAR BABY) Stanfield, he was a man only 24 years old, but more mature and experienced than most men twice his age. He has seen combat in both Afghanistan and Iraq before joining us in Blackwater. They have already written a book on the things he has done.

Arthur (ART) Laguna, one of our newest pilots, but one of the most experienced we have ever had. These BRAVE men have fought valiantly and gave the ultimate sacrifice for freedom.

Men (WARRIORS, BROTHERS IN ARMS) I hear you calling me every night in my dreams, running to me as you all did every time we received a call to go help some team in contact, saying "Boss what do you want us to do? Boss I am ready." My BROTHER in arms, this will be my last order to you, I want you to stand down, I want you to stand watch over your families until we meet again and we WILL meet again. My BROTHER WARRIORS, I will work hard to HONOR you every day by picking up the fight for freedom where you left off.

I would like to say a few remarks regarding Art. Art and I have had parallel carriers ever since we left home for the Army. Ever since I can remember Art always wanted to be a pilot. I can remember our father taking us to McClellan AFB to watch airplanes land. There would be times when we would be playing Army in our back yard and planes would fly right over our house headed for the Air Force Base; even then he would stop playing to watch it fly over.

I also remember when we were in Rio Linda Junior High School, while the rest of us would play sports, he would just stand and watch the airplanes land across the street at the Rio Linda Airport. There were many times as kids he would say, "I am going to be a pilot." I would think to myself yea right, thinking I or we would never have what it takes to be a pilot. So you can see, it has always been a dream of Art's to be a pilot. I had always thought it was an impossible dream, but Art, you showed me and many others here this day, dreams do come true.

Just like the movie Radio Flyer. Looking back at it now, you set our careers in motion, even for your nephew, my son Chris.

After graduating from flight school we went our different ways as new Army Pilots. I think Art and I thought we were the Chuck Yeager's of Army aviation. After being assigned to our first aviation unit, we both realized that wasn't true and it was going to take a lot of work just to be a good pilot. Art and I always stayed in touch through out our flying careers; letting each other know what specialty school we were headed for next.

When I put in to go to Instructor Pilot School he did the same. I soon realized Art had an ace in the hole for getting schools it was our niece Maria, who was also in the Guard and worked at Headquarters. All he had to do was call her and say, I want to go to whatever school and he would get it. I believe Art went to every school that the Army had to offer an Army pilot. Art became a Helicopter Instructor Pilot, both Army and civilian, an Army Test Pilot, an Army Aviation Safety Officer, an Army and civilian Fixed Wing Pilot. And by no stretch of the imagination are any of these courses easy, many never complete the course, but Art always excelled in each. I would get reports from my friends that were in the course with him telling me how well he was doing. Art's list of his qualifications and achievements just goes on and on.

I think we both knew some day we would work together as pilots. Shortly after I retired after thirty years from Special Operations, I went to work for another Special Group called Blackwater Aviation. I called Art and told him I was going to Iraq to fly as a civilian. If I remember right his answer was something like, "YOU ARE HUH." I knew that only meant one thing. I would probably see him there to.

Well as you guessed, one day I was sitting in our operation trailer and one of my guys opened the door and said, "Dan you have a guest." I turned around and there stood Art with a big smile on his face, as if to say you didn't think I was going to let you have all the fun by yourself did you? From that day on Art would stop in often. All the Blackwater guys really grew to like him, and told him he needed to come work with us. Well it wasn't much later I received a call from Art asking about the job with Blackwater. He did all the necessary paper work and was headed off to Blackwater training, and again he excelled.

I heard he was one of the top qualifying shooters in the course. After Art completed the course I was headed back to Iraq. Since Art had all the necessary paper work completed, together we left for his first assignment as a Blackwater Pilot. We talked at every opportunity we had catching up and sharing stories of our families. I knew Art was a great pilot and was going to be an asset to the company, but I never could have imagined the true asset he was. From the time his feet hit the ground in Baghdad, he had a smile on his face. It was so infectious guys would gather around him all the time just to talk with him. Like in everything else he soon became one of the best.

He became one of my Flight Leads in our big helicopter the Bell 412 faster than anyone did. Since he mastered that I put him in our Little Bird to fly.

He became one of the only pilots that flew both of our helicopters on missions. Anytime there was work to do he would be one of the first to volunteer for the job. The mechanics would ask for a pilot to run-up a helicopter for maintenance checks or to do a test flight and Art was the first to say I will do it. After our mechanics learned that Art had been a helicopter mechanic prior to becoming a pilot he became their best buddy.

He always found a way to not come right out and tell them what he thought was wrong and how to fix something, but rather steer them in the right direction where they came up with the solution together.

One of the best days for everyone was Aloha Fridays. We would all wear a Hawaiian shirt of some kind. When Art showed up on his first Aloha Friday with his Hawaiian shirt on, my assistant manager began to have everyone vote on Art's shirt to determine the validity of his shirt. No matter how Hawaiian, his shirt looked he always got the thumbs down on it. He must have gotten ten to fifteen Hawaiian shirts sent to him in Baghdad after that but he still received a thumbs down every Aloha Friday.

One of the pictures on display is the day I left Baghdad, to bring Art home, all the guys wanted to wear one of Art's Aloha shirts in his honor. This is another example how Art brought everyone together as a close team.

Every day Art and I had an opportunity to have some personal time together. We would walk to the GYM every morning around 0530. Whoever was done first with their work out, would wait for the other one so we could walk back together. We would always find ourselves talking about our wives and kids. Art had a great love for his family and missed them very much.

The last day we had that opportunity was 23 JAN 07, the day Art was killed in combat. That day started off like all the rest. We would get our helicopter and equipment ready to go to work. Then escort the teams on the schedule into the Red Zone. This day like so many others I received a call that a team was in contact and needed our help. I immediately launched two helicopters. Art was on one of those helicopters going out to help. As I listened to the radio within a couple of minutes we already had wounded. I immediately prepared our back-up helicopter to fly. After they dropped off their door gunner at the hospital, which had been killed, they returned to our area. I told Art and his crew that the ground team still needed our help in the Red Zone and we are taking off ASAP. Neither Art, nor his team hesitated for a second knowing what they were getting themselves back into.

Without going into any detail, Art and four others lost their lives that day trying to help others and to keep one of our VIP's safe. Just in the short time Art was with Blackwater Aviation he touched so many hearts personally and professionally. Art you will never know how I looked up to you, even though you were my little brother. There is a hole in my heart now, but it will be filled with all the wonderful memories you have left me, and all the rest of us. So now every time I fly I know you and Dad will be right there as my wing man watching over me. Arthur I salute you as a Warrior, a Hero and as my Brother in Arms. May God bless you and your family.

Dan's Letter To KSL News in Salt Lake City, Utah

Kim,

First of all, my brother is and was a HERO. All he ever wanted to do from the time I can remember as a child, was to fly. He became one of the most professional pilots you could have ever known. I recruited my brother to join us with Blackwater Aviation. We get a lot of resumes but only a few have the qualifications to join us. This is one of the most demanding jobs in Iraq. The military flies some every day but we in Blackwater Aviation are up flying in the RED zone every day all day.

To get to your question of what happened, I receive a call that we had some of our Blackwater PSD teams in contact and needed help. We are the QRF (Quick Reaction Force) for just about everyone. The military takes too long to respond because of the approval they have to get all the way up the chain of command. I am the only one that makes the decision to go or not and we always go when someone is in harms way. I sent out two helicopters to help our team in contact. After they were on station for a very short time they began to receive automatic fire. One of my door gunners was shot immediately in the head. Both helicopters flew back to the Green zone to get him to the hospital.

I was monitoring the radio and knew we had at lest one wounded. I gathered my crew together and my brother's crew then went back out to help our PSD team. When we arrived at their location, which only took about three minutes, we started to receive heavy volumes of automatic fire from all around. My brother was my wing-man at that point and as we took evasive maneuvers I heard him say they were taking rounds. By the time we had turned around he was gone.

As I continued to look for his helicopter we were also shot down.

I was able to land the helicopter in a small courtyard. I shut down the helicopter to assess the damage and to make sure my crew was ok. My crew was fine and the helicopter was shot up pretty bad but was able to fly the three to five minutes back to the Green zone. I needed to get my crew out of that area because it would have been only a few minutes before the insurgents would have gotten to us.

After I got back to the Green Zone, I had the mechanics put on three more rotor blades and went back out to find my brother and his crew. It only took them about ten to fifteen minutes to get me air borne again. I was back up looking for my brother and was able to get the military to help with the search. It took about twenty minutes to locate the helicopter. It had been shot down in a small ally, which made it very difficult to locate. By the time we found the helicopter, two of the bodies were drug out and into the street. The Army and our PSD team got there just in time before they could do anything with them.

I landed at that location so I could make sure they were my guys. When I unzipped the second body bag that the Army had already put them in, I found my brother. The ground guys told me they would get them all back to the Green zone. I walked back to my running helicopter, jumped in and flew back to the Green zone. I then realized I had to make a very difficult call to my brother's wife. I did everything I could to let her know he did not suffer and how very sorry that I was. Later that night I was asked to go to the hospital to ID my guys. Later at the hospital the U.S. Ambassador showed up to talk with me.

I am only telling you this story because I don't believe the media really tells the public how all of these Hero's, military and civilian really believe in what we are doing over here. I know we are doing the right thing in helping the Iraqi people and wish everyone could under stand that.

May God bless the men and woman here and their families.

Dan Laguna, Blackwater Aviation Program Manager, Baghdad Iraq.

Statement By Tommy Vargas

It was just like a normal day; weather was great we got our brief for the runs of the day business as usual. As a member of the Quick Reaction Force (QRF) I remember trying not to think too much into that day. Our job meant that we were to be within five minutes reaction time of all PSD teams operating in Baghdad in order to assist them should they be attacked. My first thoughts bring me to our staging area for that morning which was FOB (Forward Operating Base) Shields. Upon arrival we pulled into the gate and we staged the gun trucks in preparation for a 1 to 2 hour standby.

I was making a protein drink, talking with the guys in our truck when I heard the radio come alive with information of a team under attack. We loaded up and moved out to rescue the team when we were engaged by heavy machine guns. Our lead vehicle was damaged and the front tire was flattened. While changing the tire we received information that a Little Bird was missing.

At this time it seemed like everything just turned gray and the emotion in the truck became somber, all the faces and thoughts of who was on that Little Bird, just so many thoughts going through my mind. I knew I had to shake it off and get focused fast. I couldn't help but think; not these guys man they're the fxxxxxx best, it had to have been a set up bigger than hell. The gunners are the best, shooting on the move these pilots land atop rooftops, no way.

I was in the turret gunners' position in the follow vehicle, so I couldn't hear much traffic over the radio but the traffic I did hear made me sick to my stomach and I just wanted to get boots on the ground either to recover or help my brothers. Knowing the pilots and gunners, what weapons capabilities they had and that they would always make their rounds count, however all being equal time was not on their side. Once again all I could think about is getting there and supporting our brothers on the ground, knowing they will fight until their guns went dry.

Our team wanted to get there as fast as we could. Seemed every corner we turned in an effort to find a crash site resulted in a firefight. We would receive fire from all directions, and this continued from both sides of the street, roof tops, open windows, ground level, just ever where. This small arms fire was hitting near our trucks skipping off the ground, bouncing off the sidewalk, some shots hit our truck but nothing really major. This is because these cowards did mostly spray and pray techniques in the hope of hitting something. I recall seeing many AK-47s and just parts of forearms and hands over walls and in windows. Too bad for them the cement wasn't the strongest, which made them easy to deal with.

We drove around from street to street looking for our brothers and all I could think about was 1) there is no way we are going home without finding them and; 2) look for some sign of smoke, maybe a small firefight, the distinct sound of their weapons, the M-4, the prospect of locating them turned daunting as time ran on.

Our trucks by now had been hit numerous times, we pulled over and changed tires I believe three times, and then over the radio we heard that the Army, who had arrived to assist, had located the crash site. Our team was positioned just a few buildings down from where the U.S. Army stated the site appeared to be. During our patrol we drove threw a barrage of insurgent fire. As we tried to place our team as near as possible to the crash site it seemed as if the city has turned against us. Rounds were coming from building windows, roof tops, alley ways and the thing I recall thinking as we drove down this dark gray smoke fill street was, we must be getting close to the crash site because they are really trying to stop us from heading in this direction.

The bastards open up on us as soon as we pulled into the exact area where the U.S. Army and our downed Little Bird were. It was their strong hold, and we made it our strong hold upon arrival. I was always proud to see the Little Birds on site, just hearing them chop away when your in the shit is just a great feeling, because it's getting ready to rain lead. But this time it was a little different. As we locked down the site we received sporadic fire here, some there, just a mess, but we all kept firing, pin pointing these fxxxx and taking out as many as possible.

Then out of my left flank it was like everything stopped because a Little Bird just landed in the middle of this hell we were all in. But it did not seem to matter; rounds weren't taking this Little Bird down. Out walked the pilot of one of the fallen brothers at the time I was like this guy is nuts, furthermore he took his helmet off and tucked it under his right arm as if he was landing his bird coming home from a mission and walked to the crash site as if it was just the most pleasant day. I stopped gunning for a bit, and let the image soak in. I knew it wasn't good due to the sternness of his walk to the crash site. He seemed so determined, then the shooting started as I searched for a target in concern for that brave pilot. There was no change in his walk as I poured it on to cover him. A few minutes went by and all I could see off in the distance was our men from the team in a stack carrying body bags containing the crew. Tears filled my eyes through my goggles, and lead filled the air to cover these brave men on the ground. As we loaded up our fallen I remember Nick, our Team Leader, getting one last accountability check. We were all guns up. I took a second to glance over at that hard ass pilot, safely get back in the Little Bird and watched as he flew away with our fallen in heart and mind. It seemed as if we all flew away that day. God Bless our brothers.

These are my thoughts, which will always be an unmoving memory never forgetting this day. And I am stronger because of this day and the events that took place that evening. Everyone courageously acted as our forefathers did in past battles of our time, Leave know one behind!

Tommy Vargas

Rock Stars of Baghdad

Military.com

ON Point | Sgt Roy Batty | February 08, 2007

Copyright (c) 2010, ON Point, Reprinted with permission

There is a low buzz on the horizon, somewhere behind the buildings surrounding the tiny FOB, insectile at first, barely audible, but quickly rising on the morning breeze. At first note, you might think that it was a lawn mower, albeit one running at very high RPM, as if fueled by some lethal nitro-methane mixture.

The high tone rises steadily, fades for a moment, then soars back again, higher now, faster, and that's when we start to move outdoors, coffee cans and cigarettes in our hand, eager for the morning show. We cluster on the sandbagged patio in front of the dilapidated barracks, necks craning skyward, heads turning, looking and listening for their approach, figures around us stopped and frozen for a second on top and clustered around their HMMWVs, everybody eager.

The sound fades again for a second -- they must be behind another building -- and then increases expectantly, louder now, and I feel the anticipation in the noise, like the sound of an huge audience applauding before a show, and WROOOOOOOMMMM!!!, the tiny helicopters burst upon the stage above us, a roar and a black flash of motion 50 feet above our heads, and they're past, instantly, the sound quickly fading with the sudden doppler effect of something very loud, moving very fast.

My heart leaps into my throat as the helicopter carves a sudden, graceful arc above the compound, heeled over on it's side at an impossible 90 degree angle, roaring past the concrete edifice of the MOI building, it's stiff landing skids seemingly only a few feet from the office windows. The tiny craft pulls out of the turn and pitches straight upward, soaring into the golden blue cocktail of another Iraq morning, a children's toy rocket, heading skyward. I'm cheering now, both arms outstretched in the timeless display of victory and strength, as I do every time I see them, and I am not alone. The Rock Stars of Baghdad are here again, and another show begins!

The helicopters are Hughes Defender 500s, and they belong to Blackwater, the premier private security company in Iraq. Nobody calls them Defender 500s, though. We call them Little Birds, after the virtually identical helos flown by the Army's Night Stalkers, the 160th Special Operations Aviation Regiment. Little Birds are the sole purview of Special Forces, and particularly the legendary SFOD-D -- better known by the media's ridiculous tag -- Delta Force. CAG. The Knights Templar of American special operations.

Little Birds became famous in movies like "Black Hawk Down", and just about anything you saw them do in the movie, Blackwater's can do, too. Blackwater is, for all intents and purposes, your very own little Special Forces, available anywhere, anytime, for the low low price of a couple of million dollars. These Birds are used to fly recon and air support for various security contracts, usually with federal government agencies. Based out of the Green Zone, just a couple blocks west of here, we are fortunate enough to see them often.

None of the names or details we really care about. What matters to us is the grace and style they show in their flying, which is absolutely insane. To watch them wheel and spin, carving magnificent turns at tree top level above us, is like being treated to an air show every day. Another one buzzes toward us, that glorious whine exploding around us as it bursts from over an adjacent building, and everyone throws their heads back to watch.

Again, it is heeled over completely on it's side, and we stare in wonder at the men inside and out of it. Yes, there are guys hanging outside of it, their boots resting on the spindly skids, standing upright, their assault rifles pointing outwards. The helicopters have no doors on them, and the pilots are clearly visible, sitting back like you or I in our Laz-e-boys, while flying at God-knows-what speed and at roof top level. We always wave at them, and sometimes the new gods of the air deign to wave back at us mere mortals. The Little Bird careens wildly across the base, first jinking left, then right, and then pulling up into a sharp climbing arc, the white circle on it's rotors a blurred halo, the pitch of the wasp changing and rising as it climbs into another crazy hammerhead.

More important than the security they provide for it's convoy, the Little Birds bring a precious sense of elan, of esprit de corps, of being something elite, to our usual morning grind. You can't help but feel like you are in a really good action movie every time you see these guys, and how could you lose when you have guys and toys as cool as these on your team? The soldiers around me always say the same thing whenever Blackwater is overhead -- "Man, I would do anything to have that job!" Me, too.

A couple of weeks ago I passed one of their convoys on the way to Baghdad International Air Port, or BIAP as we call it, in yet another inevitable Army acronym. That miserable cloud-choked morning was the coldest day we've had here so far, but even with the rain and half-frozen mud, I looked at the guys huddling over the skids as they zipped overhead, and thought, "Y'know, I'd do that job for free!" And love every second of it.

It's not without it's dangers, though. Last week, one of the Blackwater Little Birds was shot down, just a few klicks north of here, in Adhamiyah, where we have had some of our own more interesting moments. Some insurgent got in a lucky shot, but even then the pilot was a consumate professional, and managed to autorotate the bird into a survivable landing. The story we heard was that they got tangled up in power lines, and came in really hard, although at least some of the pilots and crew survived the crash.

Blackwater launched their own recovery mission to rescue them, and a squad of Strykers rolled in to help, too. I would have done anything to be on that mission, but was sitting at yet another IP station a few kilometers away, just north of Sadr City. Tragically, some scumbag locals got to them first. The rescue teams found them, still strapped into the helicopter. Each man had been shot, executed without mercy, regardless of their wounds.

We all reacted the same way when we heard the tragic news. Crestfallen faces, and an emphatic, disbelieving "No way!" on our tongues. It wasn't just a machine that fell out of the sky that day, something made out of plastic and metal, a vehicle to ride in. It was that glorious leap in my heart when they roared overhead, and that instant smile they brought to my face whenever I saw them above me, sunlight glinting off their visored helmets with that suddenly sparkling prism effect. It was that sense of being part of something special.

Maybe my gunner summed it up best one day, watching them buzz our barracks for the tenth time that day, amid the throaty cheers of teenage soldiers. He shook his head, squinted up at them, and said in his Georgia drawl, "That's some sexy ***, man. That's some sexy ***."

We rode out this morning, into a daybreak that was an eery, off-world yellow. There was a monster of a sandstorm raging down in Karbala, and Baghdad was getting it's cast-off remnants. The visibility and blowing dust was so bad that our own Army helicopters were on "Red" status -- allowed to fly only in a life-or-death emergency. We were skirting through an IP checkpoint, along one of those wide and blasted city streets near Baghdad University. Cracked concrete, ancient sandbags. Rusting hulks of forgotten car bombs. Skittish dogs on the sidewalk, ribs showing. Ragged Iraqi cops in mismatched uniforms, clutching the dull brown wooden handgrips of their AKs. The usual smell of raw sewage and burning plastic.

And somewhere above the crappy morning of yet another day spent on Iraqi roads, I could hear that delicious buzz again, even from inside the armored HMMWV. Sure enough, here they came, appearing like black apparitions from the yellow muck above. They were skimming along the avenue, right in front of us, just barely above the broken streetlights, that vulpine howl rising and then breaking like a wave as they flashed over our convoy.

The rock stars were back, and the show would go on. I smiled grimly, inside my helmet, and muttered to myself. "Oh yeeaaaaah!"

It was going to be good day after all.

Blackwater's 'Little Birds' of Baghdad pack quite a sting
March 1, 2007
By Joanne Kimberlin
The Virginian-Pilot
Copyright (c) 2010, The Virginian-Pilot, Reprinted with permission

They skim the wounded skyline of an angry city - tiny black wasps, fragile yet full of sting.

Bristling with biceps and gun barrels, they're as much a part of the daily fabric of Baghdad as sandbags, checkpoints and black plumes of smoke.

They are Blackwater's Little Bird helicopters.

As icons often do, they stir emotion. The Little Birds can symbolize all that's right or wrong with the war. To the enemy, they are an evil to be struck from the sky. To an ally in trouble, their inbound buzz is the blessed sound of a second chance.

It can be much less complicated for the everyday soldier. For many grunts on the ground, Blackwater's Little Birds fill two simple needs: entertainment and inspiration.

A Marine who writes for several online publications under the pen name Sgt. Roy Batty recently shared that lens. According to editor David Danelo at ON Point, a Web site focusing on military news, Batty is deployed to Iraq and writes regularly about life in "The Sandbox." February's column was devoted to Blackwater's Little Birds.

When they come into sight, Batty wrote, he and his fellow soldiers "move outdoors, coffee cans and cigarettes in our hand, eager for the morning show."

It does not disappoint:

You Have To Live Hard To Be Hard

"My heart leaps into my throat as the helicopter carves a sudden, graceful arc above the compound, heeled over on its side at an impossible 90-degree angle... seemingly only a few feet from the office windows.

"The tiny craft pulls out of the turn and pitches straight upward.... I'm cheering now, both arms outstretched in the timeless display of victory and strength, as I do every time I see them, and I am not alone.

"The Rock Stars of Baghdad are here again, and another show begins!"

Rock stars? In the controversial, high-stakes world of private security contracting, Blackwater's men have been called plenty - everything from cold-blooded mercenaries to red-white-and-blue heroes - but nothing nearly so Hollywood.

Cue the Little Bird.

As Batty the Marine put it:

"You can't help but feel like you are in a really good action movie every time you see these guys.... How could you lose when you have guys and toys as cool as these on your team?"

Blackwater officials say "operational security concerns" prevent them from discussing the company's helicopter work. That's not surprising. Hush-hush is at the core of a big chunk of Blackwater's business: providing security in Iraq under a web of contracts.

A multimillion-dollar deal with the U.S. State Department puts the lives of diplomats and VIPs in the company's hands, including that of U.S. Ambassador Zalmay Khalilzad and just about every member of Congress who ventures into the war zone.

To do the job, the Moyock, N.C.-based outfit fields a private army of hardened men, weapons and vehicles. Wings and rotors are a critical part of the equation. None, however, turn more eyes than the handful of teardrop-shaped Little Birds that supply aerial surveillance and cover for ground convoys, ferry the occasional senior staff, and swoop in shooting when things get critical.

Stationed at LZ Washington, a landing pad inside Baghdad's Green Zone, the Little Birds are just big enough for a four-man crew. They're painted solid black with a single silver stripe. Tail numbers - customary for identification - are absent. Blackwater's bear-paw logo is nowhere to be found.

It's unclear if the company owns or leases the helos. It doesn't matter. Everyone knows who flies them - thanks in large part to their trademark door gunners.

Positioned just behind the pilot and co-pilot, tethered by "monkey harnesses," one gunner hangs out of each side of the cockpit, feet braced on the skids. With assault rifles at the ready, they dangle in mid air, scanning for the hint of an unfriendly move below.

It's a good thing they're strapped in. Their chopper was designed with maneuverability in mind.

With no heavy armor or built-in weaponry, its best defense is careening, erratic flight that's tough for the enemy to draw a bead on. Five-bladed rotors produce a here-and-gone "whir" that sounds like a whisper next to the thunderous "whup-whup-whup" of the bigger two- and three-bladed choppers. A Little Bird can hug the terrain, duck into twisted alleys and head for the sun at 3-4 feet per second.

Ron Van Sickle manages the Hampton Roads Executive Airport in Chesapeake. He's a chopper buff. He says there aren't many Little Birds in this area - either in military or civilian use - but he gets worked up just talking about the nimble craft.

"There are prettier helicopters," Van Sickle said, "but this... this is the ultimate grown man's toy. Very fast, very slick, very quiet. By the time you see it, it's too late. If you're the enemy, you're probably dead."

The Little Birds are not invincible. Like all helicopters, they're vulnerable to a single well-placed bullet from the ground, not to mention the surface-to-air missiles that sometimes turn up in the insurgent arsenal. Since May 2003, more than 60 U.S. choppers have gone down - seven in the last six weeks, most from enemy fire.

On Jan. 23, Blackwater lost its first Little Bird, and the lives of five contractors. Collectively, the men had spent roughly 80 years in uniform before going private. They were killed inside two Little Birds scrambling to cover a State Department convoy under attack. One door gunner took a bullet to the head. Four more were killed when their chopper went down under heavy fire.

Contractor deaths are often lost in the litany of war casualties. Not so with the Little Bird men. Ambassador Khalilzad, who is sometimes secreted across the city in a Little Bird, showed up at the Green Zone hospital morgue to pay his respects. Batty and his buddies grieved:

"We all reacted the same way when we heard the tragic news. Crestfallen faces, and an emphatic, disbelieving 'No way!'... It wasn't just a machine that fell out of the sky that day.... It was that sense of being part of something special."

Blackwater's "rotorheads" know the risks - and their aircraft - intimately. The company plucks many of its pilots from the Army's elite 160th Special Operations Aviation Regiment, where Little Birds figure heavily in covert warfare.

In Iraq, they are famous for pushing the chopper to its limits.

"They're very impressive pilots," said author Robert Young Pelton. "Completely fearless."

Private contracting is the subject of Pelton's book "Licensed to

Kill." He's no stranger to the sound of war drums. "The World's Most Dangerous Places" is one of his best-known works. In Iraq, he spent a month hanging out with Blackwater.

Its Little Bird pilots, he said, "do some of the most insane things I've ever seen. The most dramatic thing is when they fly at night, completely blacked out, wearing night vision goggles - and anybody who's ever looked through a pair of those knows they're limited."

Pelton said the pilots were particularly fond of buzzing a rooftop terrace at Blackwater's Baghdad compound, a popular off-duty spot for knocking back a few.

"We'd be up there drinking, in the pitch dark, and suddenly there they'd be, like 10 to 15 feet over our heads."

Pelton says the military occasionally "yells" at Blackwater for such antics. So does the State Department.

"They're sticklers for how things are done," Pelton said of the government folks. "They look at Blackwater as cowboys. Show offs."

It's a different story when bullets fly, Pelton said.

"There's not a single person over there, that if they were in a shootout, would not be relieved to see a Little Bird coming. It's like, 'Whew. Here comes the cavalry.' "

Dan Laguna says the Little Birds will come to the aid of any ally.

Laguna manages Blackwater's aviation program in Iraq. His brother, Art, was among the five killed in January. An e-mail written by Laguna to his hometown TV station in Utah shortly after the attack provides glimpses into the operation:

"We are the QRF (Quick Reaction Force) for just about everyone. The military takes too long to respond because of the approval they have to get all the way up the chain of command. I am the only one that makes the decision to go or not to go and we always go when someone is in harm's way."

Sometimes, that someone is the military itself. In recent testimony submitted to a congressional committee, Blackwater told of an incident that happened in October. Two Little Birds returning from a mission spotted an Army motorcade that had been hit by a roadside bomb.

According to the company, one helo landed so its crew could help the wounded while the other provided cover overhead. Even the Little Bird, however, is out of its element in Iraq. It was designed for low-elevation, high-speed scouting over the jungles of Vietnam.

When tapped for convoy escort in Baghdad, it's often forced into a slower orbit over urban areas where the enemy blends in with a sea of innocents.

"When taken together, that's not to the pilot's advantage," said Guy Ben-Ari, a defense industrial specialist at the Center for Strategic and International Studies in Washington. "It's a deadly combination. Literally. These aircraft were not intended to be able to withstand a lot of fire, and it only takes a moment to bring a weapon to bear."

Based on a help wanted ad Blackwater ran earlier this year, the company only intends to ratchet things up.

Placed in the Sun Journal of New Bern, N.C., a town ringed by military bases, the ad stated that Blackwater's helicopter work in Iraq is expanding. It sought pilots with service experience and mechanics to work 60-day stretches rotated with 30 days at home.

The company is already such a war zone fixture that its name has seeped into battlefield slang. When a soldier sheds his uniform to work for a private security outfit, it's known as "Going to Blackwater" - no matter the new employer.

No doubt, the cool factor of the Little Birds helps. As Batty the

Marine wrote: "The soldiers around me always say the same thing whenever Blackwater is overhead: 'Man, I would do anything to have that job.' "

In the love-'em-hate-'em universe of hired guns, Batty simply admires the Little Bird's contribution to esprit de corps in a place where morale tends to flatline fast.

Batty wrote that he didn't see a Little Bird for a week or so after January's crash. On the day they reappeared, he and his men were pushing through Baghdad in the remnants of a sandstorm. The blow had grounded the usual military choppers.

It was not a pretty scene:

"Eerie, off-world yellow.... Cracked concrete, ancient sandbags. Rusting hulks of forgotten car bombs. Skittish dogs on the sidewalk, ribs showing. Ragged Iraqi cops in mismatched uniforms... the usual smell of raw sewage and burning plastic.

"And somewhere above the crappy morning of yet another day spent on Iraqi roads, I could hear that delicious buzz again... here they came... skimming along the avenue, right in front of us, just barely above the broken streetlights....

"The rock stars were back, and the show would go on.... It was going to be a good day after all.

When Freedom Rings...

What a day! There are very few times in life when a person gets to join with "cream of the crop," "the salt of the earth" etc. This was one of those days. Hundreds of people have worked for many, many years to bring to fruition the actuality of what is know known as The Aerospace Museum of California. The dream is now a reality. It is a place of remembering...a place of legacy...a place of learning...a place of sharing and a place of memorial. I was personally proud to be shoulder to shoulder with my very favorite Rio Lindans and Elvertans and North Highlanders. I was proud of their commitment to this project. I wasn't too surprised however since these are the same people (in the audience AND on the podium) who always take time (and money) out of their day and time away from their personal lives to share so many community visions...the visions that most simply read about in the paper or see on the "news at eleven." Being there was simply an overwhelmingly being a part of history. It is very rare that there are so many important people of vision represented at one time and in one place Elected officials representatives from all branches of the service, business people, community members... heroes every one. Why? Because along with all of them were also the very young...including an entire class of students from F.C. Joyce Elementary School. The museum is about the transference of history and planting the spark of innovation and discovery in expanding young minds.

Life is not really about cute media soundbites, nor is it about short-lived political grandstands. It is about the principles of freedom. It is so eloquently encapsulated by Thomas Paine over 200 years ago with his treatise..."Common Sense." His impassioned talent for placing on paper the fervent desire of every human heart ever to desire a goodness and purpose in life, still stands as centuries old testimony of the purpose of life and the place of government.

Every politician, before burdening us with one more law, should by requirement re-read Thomas Paine. He or she needs to be reminded of their proper subservient place among the people's government. He needs to measure every new law against Thomas Paine's eloquent and divine purpose of life.

"Society in every state is a blessing, but Government, even it its best state, is but a necessary evil; in its worst state an intolerable one: for when we suffer, or are exposed to the same miseries BY A GOVERNMENT, which we might expect in a country WITHOUT GOVERNMENT, our calamity is heightened by reflecting that we furnish the means by which we suffer."

Which brings me to the next part of my day. I didn't have to wonder where the supporters of freedom were today. I didn't have to wonder where the supporters of this great country were today. I didn't have to wonder where the supporters of our community were today. They were present and accounted for at a memorial service for a fallen comrade…A hero from our community left us on January 23rd. He was doing what he loved…helping others…protecting freedom for us and for others not as fortunate as we are. Nobody forced him to do what he was doing. He did it because he believed in the same vision of the founding fathers of this country. He believed that there can be yet founding fathers in many more countries who have people who, like us, yearn to be free and have a God-given right to the same.

I depart now from my own words because there will be many who will read this with a jaundiced eye. They will be the ones who yearn to be safe…the ones who partake of the bounty but fear the sacrifice… to them, their life is of most import and sacrifice is an unknown part of speech. They are the ones who hide in the dark spaces until all is safe for a season…and spend the rest of their days tearing down those who stand firm in their principles through all seasons.

I have been ultimately fortunate in my lifetime to have shared many hours with life's heroes. Today was no exception. I counted over 1500 committed people at Arthur Laguna's memorial service. The service, almost tow and a half hours in length, praised a man who not only placed the ultimate seal on a life of service…but a man, through the testimony of the thousand and a half people attending, who was backed in principle by every one in the room.

The honors were lengthy and heartfelt. They were made especially poignant by the hundreds in uniform in the room standing at attention as each citation earned by Art Laguna was read. A citation from a president…a governor…fellow workers…fellow soldiers, fellow community members and more and more and more.

My words are trivial here because of the presence of the many peace officers. Peace officers were represented by those in the armed forces of our country, the CHP, the Sacramento County Sheriff's Department, Correctional Officers Groups, Metro Fire, Veterans groups, and service men and service women support groups.

I don't have to second guess where the heart of this country was today. It was on Elverta Road with the hearts of those who love it enough to give their all for its protection.

God bless America and the freedoms that are vouched safe within its borders that it can one day share with all the world.

Believe me…it doesn't get any more humble than this…

Keith Weber

February 2, 2007

GROM: Grupa Reagowania Operacyjno-Manewrowego "Operational Mobile Reaction Group"; (the word itself means "thunder") is the primary Special Forces unit of the Polish Land Forces. It was officially activated on 1990, and is deployed in a variety of unconventional warfare roles, including anti-terrorist actions and projection of power behind enemy lines.

The acronym GROM is also related to the name of General Gromoslaw Czempinski, whom, among other actions, managed to evacuate a number of agents and personnel from Iraq prior to the onset of Operation Desert Storm in 1991. He performed a great and heroic service to America.